A Year of Rag Quilts

For an authentic homespun look, create a cozy rag quilt or two. Made using a simple, distinctive technique, our twelve quaint wall quilts boast seasonal patterns and wonderfully textured edges. But best of all, they're easier to make than you might think! Each block is pieced and quilted separately then sewn together with the raw edges to the front. To finish, clip the edges and throw the quilt in the washing machine — it will "rag" on its own. Use the same technique with pillows or full-size quilts; our step-by-step instructions will show you how. You'll never think of "ragged" quilts in the same way again!

LEISURE ARTS, INC.
Little Rock, Arkansas

EDITORIAL STAFF

Vice President and Editor-in-Chief:
Sandra Graham Case
Executive Director of Publications:
Cheryl Nodine Gunnells
Director of Designer Relations: Debra Nettles
Senior Publications Director: Susan White Sullivan
Editorial Director: Susan Frantz Wiles
Senior Art Operations Director: Jeff Curtis
Director of Public Relations & Retail Marketing:
Stephen Wilson

PRODUCTION
Managing Editor: Cheryl R. Johnson
Senior Technical Editor: Lisa Lancaster
Technical Writer: Andrea Ahlen

EDITORIAL
Associate Editor: Kimberly L. Ross

ART
Art Publications Director:
Rhonda Hodge Shelby
Art Imaging Director: Mark Hawkins
Art Category Manager: Lora Puls
Graphic Artist: Amy Gerke
Photography Stylists: Janna Laughlin and
Sondra Daniel
Staff Photographer: Russell Ganser
Publishing Systems Administrator: Becky Riddle
Publishing Systems Assistants: Clint Hanson,
John Rose, and Chris Wertenberger

BUSINESS STAFF

Publisher: Rick Barton
Vice President, Finance: Tom Siebenmorgen
Director of Corporate Planning and Development:
Laticia Mull Dittrich
Vice President, Retail Marketing: Bob Humphrey
Vice President, Sales: Ray Shelgosh

Vice President, National Accounts: Pam Stebbins
Director of Sales and Services: Margaret Reinold
Vice President, Operations: Jim Dittrich
Comptroller, Operations: Rob Thieme
Retail Customer Service Manager: Stan Raynor
Print Production Manager: Fred F. Pruss

We have made every effort to ensure that these instructions are accurate and complete.
We cannot, however, be responsible for human error, typographical mistakes, or variations in individual work.
Made in the United States of America.

International Standard Book Number 1-57486-388-6

10   9   8   7   6

Meet Annis Clapp

Annis **C**lapp's mother always believed that her daughter was a seamstress by nature. "She says that as a child I used to sit and watch her sew," Annis admits, "but I was too young to remember."

What Annis does remember are the handmade quilts she and her eight siblings used throughout their childhood on an Idaho strawberry farm. The bedspreads were a collaborative effort — her paternal grandmother pieced the tops, and her mother lovingly quilted them.

As she grew older, Annis' love for sewing and quilting grew as well. In the 1980s Annis sold her first quilt pattern to a local company. The following decade was filled with family responsibilities that prevented her from designing much, but she still spent her spare time making and selling gift items at craft shows. Finally, in 2000, Annis entered a new season of life and started designing full-time. Her early patterns were built around quick-piecing techniques, but she didn't really find her niche until she discovered rag quilting a year later. "I knew instantly that I had a winner," she says.

Though Annis doesn't see a consistent "style" in her designs, she admits that many of her quilts incorporate a country air, perhaps drawing on experiences from her childhood. But that's not the only source from which Annis draws her inspiration.

She also loves redesigning old patterns or incorporating the newest quilting techniques with the latest patterns. In fact, she can frequently be found with a quilting magazine in hand.

And like many quilters, Annis reveals that although she enjoys the work, her favorite part of quilting is seeing the finished product. "I like things that go together quickly ... I like to see how it all comes together," she confesses.

Annis considers herself a self-taught seamstress — she gained much of her sewing and quilting knowledge through reading, asking questions, or trial and error. As such, she reminds beginning quilters not to feel boxed in by instructions. "If you can think of a better way to do something, do it. If you think you've thought of a shortcut, try it," she counsels. "Even if it doesn't work, you will learn something from it."

When she's not quilting or designing, Annis passes time with other needlecrafts such as crochet and needlepoint on plastic canvas. She also enjoys reading, designing floor plans for houses (she designed the house she and her husband built and have lived in for 26 years!), and spending time with her three children and two grandchildren.

Table of Contents

 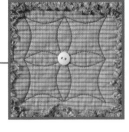
 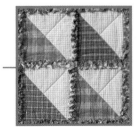

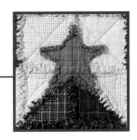

January

Finished Block Size: 5" x 5" (13 cm x 13 cm)
Finished Size (including outer fringe): 23" x 23" (58 cm x 58 cm)

$^1/_4$ yd (23 cm) of cream fabric for snowflakes
$^1/_4$ yd (23 cm) of cream print
Scrap of blue print
$^5/_8$ yd (57 cm) of blue plaid No. 1
$^1/_8$ yd (11 cm) of blue plaid No. 2
$^1/_2$ yd (46 cm) of blue plaid No. 3
$^3/_4$ yd (69 cm) **total** of 8 assorted blue plaids

$^1/_4$ yd (23 cm) of trim fabric
$^3/_8$ yd (34 cm) of fleece for batting
You will also need:
Paper-backed fusible web
Stabilizer
5 snowflake charms
   (approximately 19mm)

CUTTING OUT THE BLOCKS AND BORDERS

Refer to **Rotary Cutting**, *page 84, before beginning project.*

From cream fabric:
- Refer to **Satin Stitch Appliqué**, page 91, to use pattern, page 11, to cut 5 snowflakes (A).

From cream print:
- Cut 1 strip 2" wide. From this strip, cut 16 rectangles (B) 2" x 2$^1/_2$" for Block A.
- Cut 1 strip 3$^5/_8$" wide. From this strip, cut 8 squares (C) 3$^5/_8$" x 3$^5/_8$".

From blue print:
- Cut 1 strip 2" wide. From this strip, cut 4 squares (D) 2" x 2" for Block A.

From blue plaid No. 1:
- Cut 3 strips 6" wide. From these strips, cut 5 background squares (E) 6" x 6" for Block B and 9 squares (F) 6" x 6" for block backings.

From blue plaid No. 2:
- Cut 1 strip 3$^5/_8$" wide. From this strip, cut 8 squares (G) 3$^5/_8$" x 3$^5/_8$".

From blue plaid No. 3:
- Cut 3 strips 4$^1/_2$" wide. From these strips, cut 4 squares (H) 4$^1/_2$" x 4$^1/_2$" for Block C, 4 squares (I) 4$^1/_2$" x 4$^1/_2$" for Block C backings, and 4 rectangles (J) 4$^1/_2$" x 16" for border backings.

From assorted blue plaids:
- From **each** of 8 plaids, cut 1 strip 1$^1/_2$" wide. From **each** of 5 strips, cut 2 rectangles (K1, K2, K3, K4, or K5) 1$^1/_2$" x 20" and from **each** of 3 strips, cut 1 rectangle (K6, K7, or K8) 1$^1/_2$" x 20" for pieced borders.
- From **each** of 2 plaids, cut 1 strip 2" wide. From **each** strip, cut 1 rectangle (L1 and L2) 2" x 20" for pieced borders.
- Cut 1 rectangle (M) 8" x 21" for hanging sleeve.

From fleece:
- Cut 1 strip 4$^3/_4$" wide. From this strip, cut 9 squares (N) 4$^3/_4$" x 4$^3/_4$" for Blocks A and B.
- Cut 2 strips 3$^1/_4$" wide. From these strips, cut 4 squares (O) 3$^1/_4$" x 3$^1/_4$" for Block C and 4 rectangles (P) 14$^3/_4$" x 3$^1/_4$" for border strips.

From trim fabric:
- Cut 4 strips (Q) 1$^1/_2$" x 24".

MAKING THE BLOCKS AND BORDERS

*Each Block and Border is pieced and quilted before the quilt is assembled. Follow **Piecing and Pressing**, page 87, to make blocks.* **Note:** *Use $^1/_4$" seam allowance to piece together blocks and border strips.*

Block A

1. Draw a diagonal line (corner to corner) on **wrong** side of each cream square (C). With right sides together, place a cream square (C) on top of a No. 2 blue plaid square (G). Stitch seam $^1/_4$" from each side of drawn line (**Fig. 1**).

Fig. 1

2. Cut along drawn line and press open to make 2 triangle-squares. Trim $^1/_8$" from the cream sides and $^5/_8$" from the blue sides of each triangle-square (**Fig. 2**) to make a **Unit 1** square ($2^1/_2$" x $2^1/_2$"). Make 16 **Unit 1's**.

Fig. 2

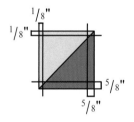

Unit 1
(make 16)

3. Sew 2 **Unit 1's** and a cream rectangle (B) together as shown to make **Unit 2**. Make 8 **Unit 2's**.

Unit 2
(make 8)

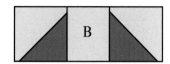

4. Sew 2 cream rectangles (B) and a blue print square (D) together as shown to make **Unit 3**. Make 4 **Unit 3's**.

Unit 3
(make 4)

5. Sew 2 **Unit 2's** and a **Unit 3** together as shown to make **Block A**. Make 4 **Block A's**.

Block A Diagram
(make 4)

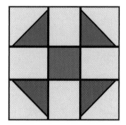

6. Follow **Quilting Instructions**, page 90, to layer backing square (F), fleece square (N), and **Block A** together. Quilt "in-the-ditch" along each seam to complete the block.

8

Block B

1.   Follow **Satin Stitch Appliqué**, page 91, to center and fuse snowflake (A) to No. 1 blue plaid background square (E) to make **Block B**. Make 5 **Block B's**.

Block B Diagram
(make 5)

2.   Follow **Quilting Instructions**, page 90, to layer backing square (F), fleece square (N), and **Block B** together.
3.   Machine appliqué snowflake in place through all layers to complete the block.

Block C

1.   Follow **Quilting Instructions**, page 90, to mark and layer No. 3 blue plaid backing square (I), fleece square (O), and No. 3 blue plaid square (H) together. Quilt with an X to complete **Block C**. Make 4 **Block C's**.

Block C Diagram
(make 4)

Pieced Border Strips

1.   Sew 2 strips (L1 and L2) and 13 strips (K1-K8) together as shown to make **Strip Set**.

Strip Set

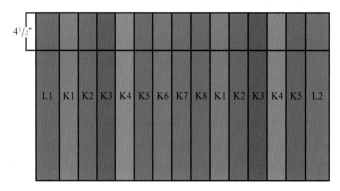

2.   Cut across **Strip Set** at $4^{1}/_{2}$" intervals to make **Unit 4**. Make 4 **Unit 4's**.

Unit 4
(make 4)

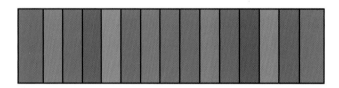

3.   Follow **Quilting Instructions**, page 90, to layer No. 3 blue plaid backing rectangle (J), fleece rectangle (P), and **Unit 4** together. Quilt "in-the-ditch" along each seam to complete the pieced border strips.

ASSEMBLING THE QUILT

*As the quilt is assembled, the rag seams are created on the front of the quilt by sewing the blocks and borders together with back sides together. Refer to **Assembling The Quilt**, page 88, for additional information. Use $^1/_2"$ seam allowance to assemble quilt.*

1. Sew 1 **Block A** and 2 **Block B's** together as shown to make **Unit 5**. Make 2 **Unit 5's**.

Unit 5
(make 2)

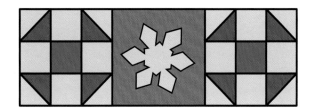

2. Sew 2 **Block A's** and 1 **Block B** together as shown to make **Unit 6**.

Unit 6

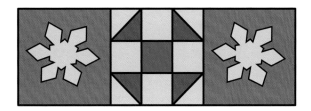

3. Sew 2 **Unit 5's** and a **Unit 6** together to make **Unit 7**.

Unit 7

4. Sew a **Unit 4** to each side of **Unit 7**.
5. Sew a **Block C** to each end of a **Unit 4** to make **Unit 8**. Make 2 **Unit 8's**.

Unit 8
(make 2)

6. Sew **Unit 8's** to top and bottom of **Unit 7**.

COMPLETING THE QUILT

Refer to page 89 for Steps 1-3.

1. Make and attach a hanging sleeve (M) to back of quilt.
2. Sew trim strips (Q) to edges of quilt.
3. Fringe rag seams. Wash and dry quilt.
4. Sew a snowflake charm to center of each Block B using clear nylon thread.

Quilt Diagram

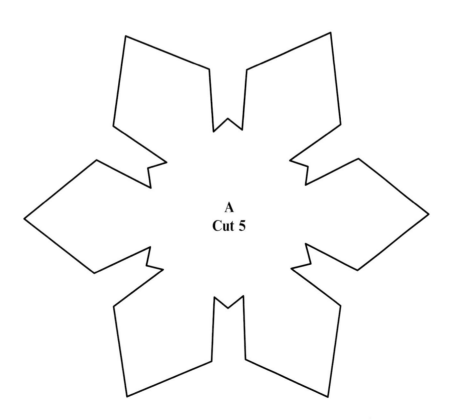

A
Cut 5

February

Finished Block Size: 5$\frac{1}{2}$" x 5$\frac{1}{2}$" (14 cm x 14 cm)
Finished Size (including outer fringe): 23$\frac{1}{2}$" x 23$\frac{1}{2}$" (60 cm x 60 cm)

$^1/_2$ yd (46 cm) of cream fabric
$^1/_4$ yd (23 cm) red plaid No. 1
$^3/_8$ yd (34 cm) red plaid No. 2
$^1/_4$ yd (23 cm) red plaid No. 3
$^5/_8$ yd (57 cm) red plaid No. 4

$^1/_4$ yd (23 cm) of trim fabric
$^1/_2$ yd (46 cm) of fleece for batting
You will also need:
 Paper-backed fusible web

CUTTING OUT THE BLOCKS AND BORDERS

*Refer to **Rotary Cutting**, page 84, before beginning project.*

From cream fabric:
- Cut 2 strips 6$^1/_2$" wide. From these strips, cut 4 squares (A) 6$^1/_2$" x 6$^1/_2$" for Block B and 4 squares (B) 6$^1/_2$" x 6$^1/_2$" for Block B backings.
- Cut 1 strip 3$^1/_2$" wide. From this strip, cut 2 rectangles (C) 15" x 3$^1/_2$" for Block C.

From red plaid No. 1:
- Use pattern, page 17, to cut 8 hearts (D).

From red plaid No. 2:
- Cut 1 strip 6$^1/_2$" wide. From this strip, cut 1 square (E) 6$^1/_2$" x 6$^1/_2$" for Block A and 5 squares (F) 6$^1/_2$" x 6$^1/_2$" for Block A and C backings.
- Cut 1 strip (G1) 15" x 3$^1/_2$" for Block C.

From red plaid No. 3:
- Cut 1 strip (G2) 15" x 3$^1/_2$" for Block C.
- Cut 1 strip 4" wide. From this strip, cut 4 squares (H) 4" x 4" for Block D and 4 squares (I) 4" x 4" for Block D backings.

From red plaid No. 4:
- Cut 4 strips 4" wide. From these strips, cut 4 rectangles (J) 17$^1/_2$" x 4" for Block E and 4 rectangles (K) 17$^1/_2$" x 4" for Block E backings.
- Cut 1 rectangle (L) 21$^1/_2$" x 3$^1/_2$" for hanging sleeve.

From fleece:
- Cut 2 strips 5$^1/_4$" wide. From these strips, cut 9 squares (M) 5$^1/_4$" x 5$^1/_4$" for Blocks A, B, and C.
- Cut 2 strips 2$^3/_4$" wide. From these strips, cut 4 squares (N) 2$^3/_4$" x 2$^3/_4$" for Block D and 4 rectangles (O) 16$^1/_4$" x 2$^3/_4$" for Block E.

From trim fabric:
- Cut 4 strips (P) 1$^1/_2$" x 24".

MAKING THE BLOCKS AND BORDERS

*Each Block and Border is pieced and quilted before the quilt is assembled. Follow **Piecing and Pressing**, page 87, to make blocks.*

Block A

1. Follow **Quilting Instructions**, page 90, to mark No. 2 red plaid square (E) using **Template 1**, page 17.
2. Layer No. 2 red plaid backing square (F), fleece square (M), and No. 2 red plaid square (E) together. Quilt using a contrasting color thread to make **Block A**.

Block A Diagram

Block B

1. Follow **Frayed-Edge Appliqué**, page 91, to make **Block B** using 2 hearts (D), cream backing square (B), cream square (A), and fleece square (M). Make 4 **Block B's**.

Block B Diagram
(make 4)

Block C

Note: Use ¹/₄" seam allowance to piece blocks.

1. Sew 1 cream rectangle (C) and 1 No. 2 red plaid rectangle (G1) together as shown to make **Strip Set A**. Repeat with rectangles C and G2 to make **Strip Set B**.

Strip Set A

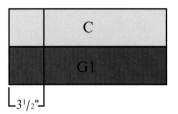

Strip Set B

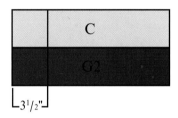

Cut across **Strip Set A** and **Strip Set B** at 3¹/₂" intervals to make **Unit 1** and **Unit 2**. Make 4 **Unit 1's** and 4 **Unit 2's**.

Unit 1
(make 4)

Unit 2
(make 4)

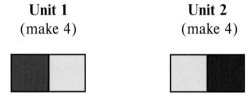

2. Sew a **Unit 1** and **Unit 2** together as shown to make **Block C**. Make 4 **Block C's**.

Block C Diagram
(make 4)

3. Follow **Quilting Instructions**, page 90, to layer No. 2 red plaid backing square (F), fleece square (M), and **Block C**.

4. Quilt each block with an X and "in-the-ditch" along each seam.

Block D

1. Follow **Quilting Instructions**, page 90, to mark No. 3 red plaid square (H) using **Template 2**, page 17.

2. Layer No. 3 red plaid backing square (I), fleece square (N), and No. 3 red plaid square (H) together. Quilt using a contrasting color thread to make **Block D**. Make 4 **Block D's**.

Block D Diagram
(make 4)

Block E

1. Follow **Quilting Instructions**, page 90, to mark No. 4 red plaid rectangle (J) using **Template 3**, page 17.

2. Layer No. 4 red plaid backing rectangle (K), fleece rectangle (O), and No. 4 red plaid rectangle (J) together. Quilt using a contrasting color thread to make **Block E**. Make 4 **Block E's**.

Block E Diagram
(make 4)

ASSEMBLING THE QUILT

As the quilt is assembled, the rag seams are created on the front of the quilt by sewing the blocks and borders together with back sides together. Refer to **Assembling The Quilt**, *page 88, for additional information. Use* ¹/₂" *seam allowance to assemble quilt.*

1. Sew a **Block B** and 2 **Block C's** together as shown to make **Unit 3**. Make 2 **Unit 3's**.

Unit 3
(make 2)

2. Sew a **Block A** and 2 **Block B's** together as shown to make **Unit 4**.

Unit 4

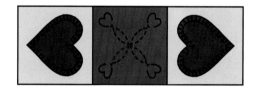

3. Sew 2 **Unit 3's** and a **Unit 4** together to make quilt center.

4. Sew a **Block E** to each side of quilt center.

5. Sew a **Block D** to each end of a **Block E** to make **Unit 5**. Make 2 **Unit 5's**.

Unit 5
(make 2)

6. Sew a **Unit 5** to the top and bottom of quilt center.

COMPLETING THE QUILT

Refer to page 89 for Steps 1-3.

1. Make and attach a hanging sleeve (L) to back of quilt.

2. Sew trim strips (P) to edges of quilt.

3. Fringe rag seams. Wash and dry quilt.

Quilt Diagram

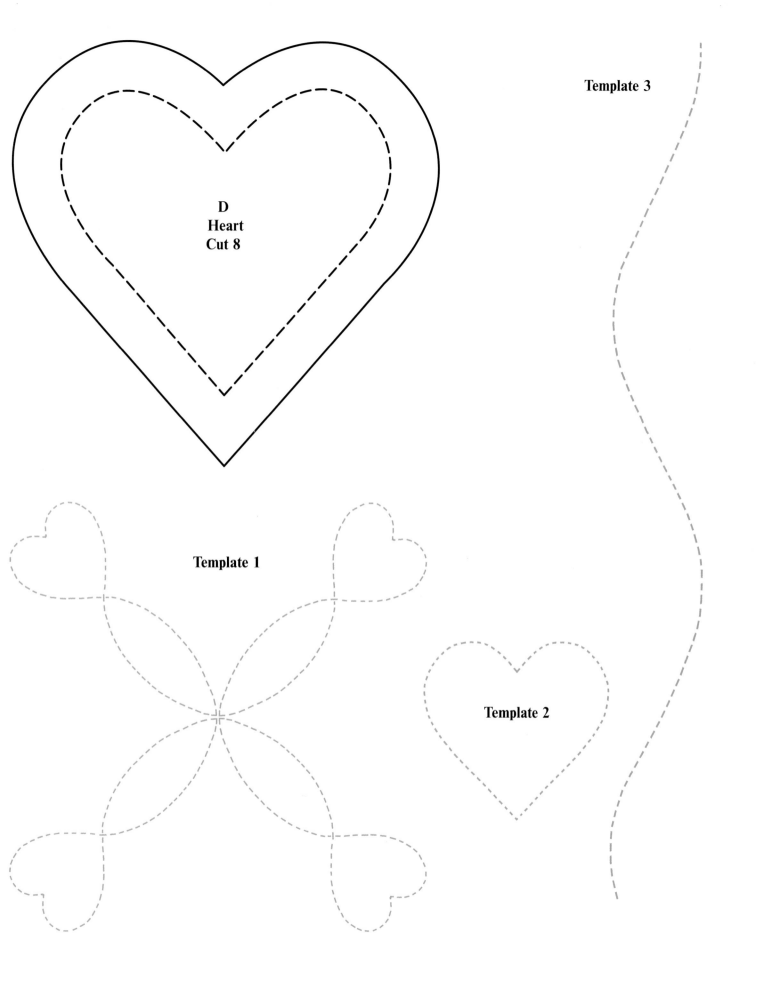

D
Heart
Cut 8

Template 3

Template 1

Template 2

March

Finished Block Size: 6" x 6" (15 cm x 15 cm)
Finished Size (including outer fringe): 25" x 25" (64 cm x 64 cm)

1³/₈ yds (1.3 m) of beige plaid
¹/₈ yd (11 cm) of green plaid No. 1
¹/₂ yd (46 cm) of green plaid No. 2
³/₈ yd (34 cm) of green plaid No. 3
¹/₂ yd (46 cm) of green plaid No. 4

¹/₄ yd (23 cm) of trim fabric
¹/₂ yd (46 cm) of fleece for batting
You will also need:
   Paper-backed fusible web
   Stabilizer

CUTTING OUT THE BLOCKS

*Refer to **Rotary Cutting**, page 84, before beginning project.*

From beige plaid:
- Cut 3 strips 4¹/₄" wide. From these strips, cut 20 squares (A) 4¹/₄" x 4¹/₄" for Block A.
- Cut 4 strips 2¹/₄" wide. From these strips, cut 2 rectangles (B) 15" x 2¹/₄" for Block B, 1 rectangle (C) 30" x 2¹/₄" for Block C, and 1 rectangle (D) 38" x 2¹/₄" for Block C.
- Cut 1 strip 3¹/₂" wide. From this strip, cut 1 rectangle (E) 20" x 3¹/₂" for Block B.
- Cut 1 strip 4³/₈" wide. From this strip, cut 6 squares (F) 4³/₈" x 4³/₈" for Block D.
- Cut 2 strips 7" wide. From these strips, cut 4 squares (G) 7" x 7" for Block B backing and 8 rectangles (H) 7" x 4" for Block C backing.

From green plaid No. 1:
- Refer to **Satin Stitch Appliqué**, page 91, to use pattern, page 23, to cut 3 shamrocks; cut 2 in reverse (I).

From green plaid No. 2:
- Cut 2 strips 7" wide. From these strips, cut 5 squares (J) 7" x 7" for Block A center and 5 squares (K) 7" x 7" for Block A backing.

From green plaid No. 3:
- Cut 1 strip 3¹/₂" wide. From this strip, cut 1 rectangle (L) 15" x 3¹/₂" for Block B and 4 rectangles (M) 3¹/₂" x 6" for hanging tabs.
- Cut 4 strips 2¹/₄" wide. From these strips, cut 2 rectangles (N) 20" x 2¹/₄" for Block B, 1 rectangle (O) 30" x 2¹/₄" for Block C, and 1 rectangle (P) 38" x 2¹/₄" for Block C.

From green plaid No. 4:
- Cut 1 strip 4³/₈" wide. From this strip, cut 6 squares (Q) 4³/₈" x 4³/₈" for Block D.
- Cut 2 strips 4" wide. From these strips, cut 12 squares (R) 4" x 4" for Block D backings.

From fleece:
- Cut 2 strips 5³/₄" wide. From these strips, cut 9 squares (S) 5³/₄" x 5³/₄" for Blocks A and B and 8 rectangles (T) 5³/₄" x 2³/₄" for Block C.
- Cut 1 strip 2³/₄" wide. From this strip, cut 12 squares (U) 2³/₄" x 2³/₄" for Block D.

From trim fabric:
- Cut 4 strips (V) 1¹/₂" x 26".

MAKING THE BLOCKS

*Each Block is pieced and quilted before the quilt is assembled. Follow **Piecing and Pressing**, page 87, to make blocks. **Note:** Use $^1/_4$" seam allowance to piece together blocks.*

Block A

1. Draw a diagonal line (corner to corner) on wrong side of each beige plaid square (A). With right sides together, place a beige plaid square (A) on top of a No. 2 green plaid square (J). Stitch seam on drawn line (**Fig. 1**). Trim seam allowance to $^1/_4$". Press seam towards triangle (**Fig. 2**). Repeat for 3 remaining corners to make background block (**Fig. 3**).

Fig. 1

Fig. 2

Fig. 3

2. Center and fuse shamrock appliqué (I) to background block.

3. Follow **Quilting Instructions**, page 90, to mark block diagonally on each corner triangle.

4. Layer No. 2 green plaid backing square (K), fleece square (S), and block together. Quilt "in-the-ditch" along each seam and diagonally on each triangle (**Fig. 4**).

Fig. 4

5. Follow **Satin Stitch Appliqué**, page 91, to appliqué shamrock in place through all layers to make **Block A**. Make 5 **Block A's**.

Block A Diagram
(make 5)

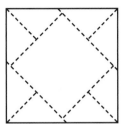

Block B

1. Sew 2 beige plaid rectangles (B) and 1 No. 3 green plaid rectangle (L) together as shown to make **Strip Set A**.

Strip Set A

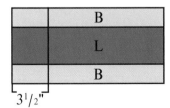

20

Cut across **Strip Set A** at $3^1/2$" intervals to make **Unit 1**. Make 4 **Unit 1's**.

Unit 1
(make 4)

2. Sew 2 No. 3 green plaid rectangles (N) and 1 beige plaid rectangle (E) together as shown to make **Strip Set B**.

Strip Set B

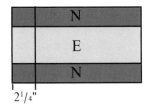

Cut across **Strip Set B** at $2^1/4$" intervals to make **Unit 2**. Make 8 **Unit 2's**.

Unit 2
(make 8)

3. Sew a **Unit 1** and 2 **Unit 2's** together to make **Block B**. Make 4 **Block B's**.

Block B Diagram
(make 4)

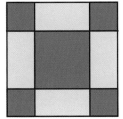

4. Follow **Quilting Instructions**, page 90, to layer beige plaid backing square (G), fleece square (S), and **Block B** together. Quilt "in-the-ditch" along each seam.

Block C

1. Sew 1 beige plaid rectangle (C) and 1 No. 3 green plaid rectangle (O) together as shown to make **Strip Set C**.

Strip Set C

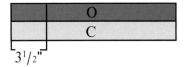

Cut across **Strip Set C** at $3^1/2$" intervals to make **Unit 3**. Make 8 **Unit 3's**.

Unit 3
(make 8)

2. Sew 1 beige plaid rectangle (D) and 1 No. 3 green plaid rectangle (P) together as shown to make **Strip Set D**.

Strip Set D

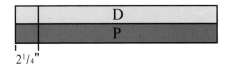

Cut across **Strip Set D** at $2^1/4$" intervals to make **Unit 4**. Make 16 **Unit 4's**.

Unit 4
(make 16)

3. Sew a **Unit 3** and 2 **Unit 4's** together as shown to make **Block C**. Make 8 **Block C's**.

Block C Diagram
(make 8)

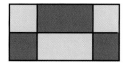

4. Follow **Quilting Instructions**, page 90, to layer beige plaid backing rectangle (H), fleece rectangle (T), and **Block C** together. Quilt "in-the-ditch" along each seam.

Block D

1. Draw a diagonal line (corner to corner) on wrong side of each beige plaid square (F). With right sides together, place a beige plaid square (F) on top of a No. 4 green plaid square (Q). Stitch seam $1/4$" from each side of drawn line (**Fig. 5**).

Fig. 5

2. Cut along drawn line and press open to make 2 **Block D's**. Repeat with remaining squares to make 12 **Block D's**.

Block D
(make 12)

3. Follow **Quilting Instructions**, page 90, to layer No. 4 green plaid backing square (R), fleece square (U), and **Block D** together. Quilt **Block D** diagonally as shown in **Fig. 6**.

Fig. 6

ASSEMBLING THE QUILT

*As the quilt is assembled, the rag seams are created on the front of the quilt by sewing the blocks and borders together with back sides together. Refer to **Assembling The Quilt**, page 88, for additional information. Use $1/2$" seam allowance to assemble quilt.*

1. Sew 2 **Block A's**, 2 **Block C's** and 1 **Block B** together as shown to make **Unit 5**. Make 2 **Unit 5's**.

Unit 5
(make 2)

2. Sew 4 **Block D's**, 2 **Block B's** and 1 **Block A** together as shown to make **Unit 6**.

Unit 6

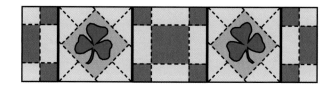

3. Sew 4 **Block D's** and 2 **Block C's** together as shown to make **Unit 7**. Make 2 **Unit 7's**.

Unit 7
(make 2)

4. Sew 2 **Unit 5's**, a **Unit 6**, and 2 **Unit 7's** together as shown.

COMPLETING THE QUILT

Refer to page 89 for Steps 1-3.

1. Using No. 3 green plaid rectangles (M), make and attach 4 hanging tabs to back of quilt.

2. Sew trim strips (V) to edges of quilt.

3. Fringe rag seams. Wash and dry quilt.

Quilt Diagram

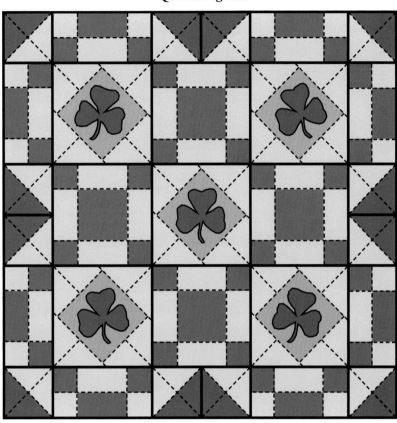

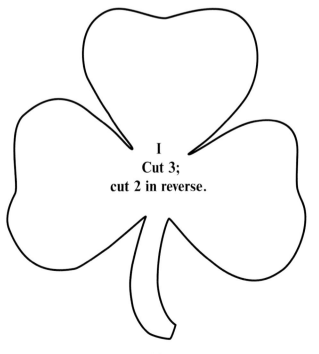

I
Cut 3;
cut 2 in reverse.

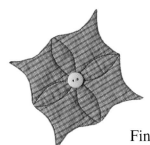

April

Finished Block Size: 5" x 5" (13 cm x 13 cm)
Finished Size (including outer fringe): 23" x 23" (58 cm x 58 cm)

Yardage is based on 45"w fabric.

$^3/_8$ yd (34 cm) of cream fabric
$^5/_8$ yd (57 cm) of lavender plaid No. 1
$^1/_4$ yd (23 cm) of lavender plaid No. 2
$^5/_8$ yd (57 cm) of lavender plaid No. 3

$^3/_8$ yd (34 cm) of green plaid
$^1/_4$ yd (23 cm) of trim fabric
$^3/_8$ yd (34 cm) of fleece for batting
Five $^5/_8$" (16 mm) dia. cream buttons

CUTTING OUT THE BLOCKS AND BORDERS

*Refer to **Rotary Cutting**, page 84, before beginning project.*

From cream fabric:
- Cut 2 strips $3^3/_4$" wide. From these strips, cut 8 squares (A) $3^3/_4$" x $3^3/_4$" for Block B and 8 squares (B) $3^3/_4$" x $3^3/_4$" for Block C.
- Cut 2 strips $1^1/_2$" wide. From these strips, cut 4 rectangles (C) 16" x $1^1/_2$" for Block E.

From lavender plaid No. 1:
- Cut 1 strip 6" wide. From this strip, cut 1 square (D) 6" x 6" for Block A and 1 square (E) 6" x 6" for Block A backing.
- Cut 2 strips $4^1/_2$" wide. From these strips, cut 4 rectangles (F) 16" x $4^1/_2$" for Block E backing.
- Cut 1 rectangle (G) 21" x 4" for hanging sleeve.

From lavender plaid No. 2:
- Cut 1 strip 6" wide. From this strip, cut 4 squares (H) 6" x 6" for Block B.

From lavender plaid No. 3:
- Cut 1 strip 6" wide. From this strip, cut 4 squares (I) 6" x 6" for Block B backing.
- Cut 1 strip $4^1/_2$" wide. From this strip, cut 4 squares (J) $4^1/_2$" x $4^1/_2$" for Block D backing.
- Cut 4 strips 2" wide. From these strips, cut 8 rectangles (K) 16" x 2" for Block E.

From green plaid:
- Cut 2 strips 6" wide. From these strips, cut 4 squares (L) 6" x 6" for Block C and 4 squares (M) 6" x 6" for Block C backing.

From fleece:
- Cut 1 strip $4^3/_4$" wide. From this strip, cut 9 squares (N) $4^3/_4$" x $4^3/_4$" for Blocks A, B, and C.
- Cut 2 strips $3^1/_4$" wide. From these strips, cut 4 squares (O) $3^1/_4$" x $3^1/_4$" for Block D and 4 rectangles (P) $14^3/_4$" x $3^1/_4$" for Block E.

From trim fabric:
- Cut 4 strips (Q) $1^1/_2$" x 24".

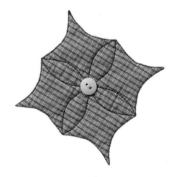

MAKING THE BLOCKS AND BORDERS

*Each Block and Border is pieced and quilted before the quilt is assembled. Follow **Piecing and Pressing**, page 87, to make blocks. **Note:** Use ¹/₄" seam allowance to piece together blocks and border strips.*

Block A

1. Follow **Quilting Instructions**, page 90, to mark No. 1 lavender plaid square (D) using **Template**, page 29.
2. Layer No. 1 lavender plaid backing square (E), fleece square (N), and No. 1 lavender plaid square (D) together. Quilt with a triple stitch using a contrasting color thread to make **Block A**.

Block A Diagram

> **Tip:** A triple stitch is a machine stitch that is formed by stitching forward several stitches and then backward. This creates a heavier line of stitching that is actually 3 closely spaced parallel lines.

Block B

1. Draw a diagonal line (corner to corner) on wrong side of each cream square (A). With right sides together and matching raw edges, place a cream square (A) on top of a No. 2 lavender plaid square (H). Stitch seam on **drawn line**; stitch again ¹/₂" from seam (**Fig. 1**). Cut halfway between seams, making a triangle-square (R) that will be used for **Block D**. Press.

Fig. 1

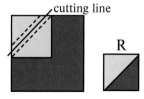

cutting line

R

2. Sew a second cream square (A) to No. 2 lavender plaid square (H) to make **Block B**. Make 4 **Block B's**.

Block B Diagram
(make 4)

3. Follow **Quilting Instructions**, page 90, to layer No. 3 lavender plaid backing square (I), fleece square (N), and **Block B** together. Quilt as shown in **Fig. 2**.

Fig. 2

Block C

1. Refer to **Block B**, Step 1 to sew 2 cream squares (B) to opposite corners of a green plaid square (L) (**Fig. 3**) to make **Block C**. The triangle-squares (S) made will be used for **Block D**. Make 4 **Block C's**.

Fig. 3

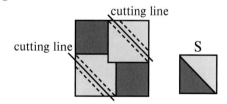

cutting line

cutting line

S

Block C Diagram
(make 4)

2. Follow **Quilting Instructions**, page 90, to layer green plaid backing square (M), fleece square (N), and **Block C** together. Quilt as shown in **Fig. 4**.

Fig. 4

3. Press open the 16 triangle-squares (R and S) leftover from **Blocks B** and **C**. Trim each triangle-square $1/2$" from both plaid edges (**Fig. 5**) so that triangle-squares measure $2^1/2$" x $2^1/2$".

Fig. 5

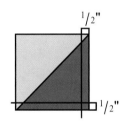

4. Sew an R and S triangle-square together as shown to make **Unit 1**. Make 8 **Unit 1's**.

Unit 1
(make 8)

5. Sew 2 **Unit 1's** together as shown to make **Block D**. Make 4 **Block D's**.

Block D Diagram
(make 4)

6. Follow **Quilting Instructions**, page 90, to layer No. 3 lavender plaid backing square (J), fleece square (O), and **Block D**. Quilt "in-the-ditch" along each seam to complete the block.

Block E

1. For one-step piecing and quilting, layer No. 1 lavender plaid backing (F), wrong side facing up, and fleece rectangle (P) together. Center cream rectangle (C), with right side facing up, on top of the fleece and pin in place (**Fig. 6**).

Fig. 6

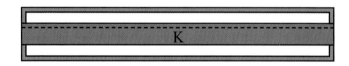

2. With right sides together and raw edges even, place a No. 3 lavender plaid rectangle (K) on cream rectangle (C) and sew together through all layers (**Fig. 7**). Press lavender rectangle toward outer edge. Repeat with second No. 3 lavender plaid rectangle (K) to make **Block E**. Make 4 **Block E's**.

Fig. 7

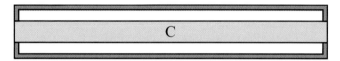

Block E Diagram
(make 4)

K
C
K

ASSEMBLING THE QUILT

*As the quilt is assembled, the rag seams are created on the front of the quilt by sewing the blocks and borders together with back sides together. Refer to **Assembling The Quilt**, page 88, for additional information. Use $^1/_2$" seam allowance to assemble quilt.*

1. Sew 2 **Block C's** and a **Block B** together as shown to make **Unit 2**. Make 2 **Unit 2's**.

Unit 2

(make 2)

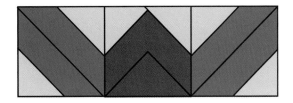

2. Sew **Block A** and 2 **Block B's** together as shown to make **Unit 3**.

Unit 3

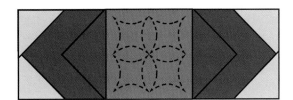

3. Sew 2 **Unit 2's** and a **Unit 3** together to make quilt center.
4. Sew a **Block E** to each side of quilt center.
5. Sew a **Block D** to each end of a **Block E** to make **Unit 4**. Make 2 **Unit 4's**.

Unit 4

(make 2)

6. Sew a **Unit 4** to the top and bottom of quilt center.

COMPLETING THE QUILT

Refer to page 89 for Steps 1-3.

1. Make and attach a hanging sleeve (G) to back of quilt.
2. Sew trim strips (Q) to edges of quilt.
3. Fringe rag seams. Wash and dry quilt.
4. Sew buttons to centers of **Blocks A** and **D**.

Quilt Diagram

Template

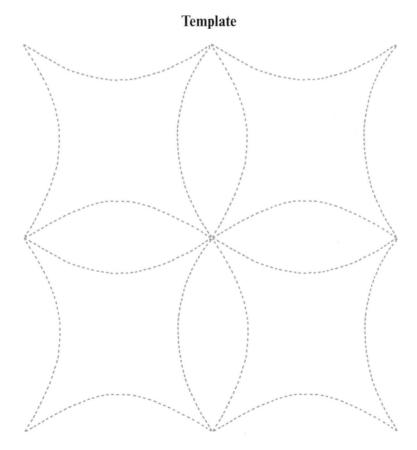

May

Finished Block Size: $7\frac{1}{2}$" x $7\frac{1}{2}$" (19 cm x 19 cm)
Finished Size (including outer fringe): 22" x 22" (56 cm x 56 cm)

$^1/_2$ yd (46 cm) of cream fabric
18" x 22" (46 cm x 56 cm) piece of
  floral print
$^1/_4$ yd (23 cm) of blue print No. 1
$^1/_4$ yd (23 cm) of blue print No. 2
$1^1/_4$ yds (1.1 m) of blue plaid

Scraps of pink and green plaids
$^1/_4$ yd (23 cm) of trim fabric
$^5/_8$ yd (57 cm) of fleece for batting
You will also need:
One $^3/_4$" (19 mm) dia. button
Paper-backed fusible web

CUTTING OUT THE BLOCKS

*Refer to **Rotary Cutting**, page 84, before beginning project.*

From cream fabric:
- Cut 1 square (A) $8^1/_2$" x $8^1/_2$" for Block A.
- Cut 2 strips $2^3/_4$" wide. From these strips, cut 8 squares (B) $2^3/_4$" x $2^3/_4$" and 8 rectangles (C) $4^1/_2$" x $2^3/_4$".
- Cut 1 strip $3^3/_8$" wide. From this strip, cut 12 squares (D) $3^3/_8$" x $3^3/_8$".

From floral print:
- Cut 1 strip $4^5/_8$" wide. From this strip, cut 2 squares (E) $4^5/_8$" x $4^5/_8$".

From blue print No. 1:
- Cut 1 square (F) $4^5/_8$" x $4^5/_8$".
- Cut 1 strip $3^3/_8$" wide. From this strip, cut 6 squares (G) $3^3/_8$" x $3^3/_8$".

From blue print No. 2:
- Cut 1 square (H) $4^5/_8$" x $4^5/_8$".
- Cut 1 strip $3^3/_8$" wide. From this strip, cut 6 squares (I) $3^3/_8$" x $3^3/_8$".

From blue plaid:
- Cut 2 strips $8^1/_2$" wide. From these strips, cut 5 squares (J) $8^1/_2$" x $8^1/_2$" for Block A, B1, and B2 backings.
- Cut 1 strip $9^1/_8$" wide. From this strip, cut 4 squares $9^1/_8$" x $9^1/_8$". Cut each square once diagonally to make 4 side setting triangles (K) and 4 backings (L).

- Cut 1 strip 10" wide. From this strip, cut 2 squares 10" x 10". Cut each square twice diagonally to make 4 corner setting triangles (M) and 4 backings (N).
- Use pattern, page 36, to cut 2 flower centers (O).
- Cut 1 rectangle (P) 20" x 8" for hanging sleeve.

From pink plaid:
- Use pattern, page 36, to cut 2 flowers (Q).

From green plaid:
- Use pattern, page 36, to cut 8 leaves (R).

From fleece:
- Cut 1 strip $7^1/_4$" wide. From this strip, cut 5 squares (S) $7^1/_4$" x $7^1/_4$" for blocks.
- Cut 1 strip $7^1/_8$" wide. From this strip, cut 2 squares $7^1/_8$" x $7^1/_8$". Cut each square once diagonally to make 4 triangles (T) for side setting triangles.
- Cut 1 square $6^7/_8$" x $6^7/_8$". Cut square twice diagonally to make 4 triangles (U) for corner setting triangles.

From trim fabric:
- Cut 4 strips (V) $1^1/_2$" x 23".

MAKING THE BLOCKS

*Each Block is pieced and quilted before the quilt is assembled. Follow **Piecing and Pressing**, page 87, to make blocks. **Note:** Use 1/4" seam allowance to piece together blocks.*

Block A

1. Follow **Frayed-Edge Appliqué**, page 91, to make **Block A** using 8 leaves (R), 2 flowers (Q), 2 flower centers (O), cream square (A), blue plaid backing square (J), and fleece square (S).

Block A Diagram

Block B

1. Draw a diagonal line (corner to corner) on wrong side of each cream square (D). With right sides together, place a cream square (D) on top of a No. 1 blue print square (G). Stitch seam 1/4" from each side of drawn line (**Fig. 1**).

Fig. 1

2. Trim along drawn line and press open to make 2 **Unit 1** triangle-squares. Make 12 **Unit 1's**.

Unit 1
(make 12)

3. Repeat with a cream square (D) and a No. 2 blue print square (I) to make 12 **Unit 2** triangle-squares.

Unit 2
(make 12)

4. Positioning triangle-squares as shown in **Fig. 2**, trim 1/8" from each cream side and bottom blue print side and 5/8" from right blue print side of 6 **Unit 1's** and 6 **Unit 2's** to make **Unit 3** and **Unit 4** rectangles (2 1/4" x 2 3/4").

Fig. 2

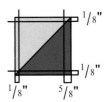

Unit 3
(make 6)

Unit 4
(make 6)

5. Positioning remaining triangle-squares as shown in **Fig. 3**, trim 1/8" from **each** cream side and bottom blue print side and 5/8" from left blue print side of 6 **Unit 1's** and 6 **Unit 2's** to make **Unit 5** and **Unit 6** rectangles (2 1/4" x 2 3/4").

Fig. 3

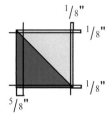

Unit 5
(make 6)

Unit 6
(make 6)

6. Repeat Steps 1 and 2 using floral print squares (E) and No. 1 and No. 2 blue print squares (F and H) to make 2 **Unit 7** triangle-squares and 2 **Unit 8** triangle-squares. Trim each triangle-square to measure 4" x 4".

Unit 7
(make 2)

Unit 8
(make 2)

7. Sew 2 **Unit 3's** together as shown to make **Unit 9**. Make 2 **Unit 9's**.

Unit 9
(make 2)

8. Sew 2 **Unit 5's** and a cream square (B) together as shown to make **Unit 10**. Make 2 **Unit 10's**.

Unit 10
(make 2)

9. Sew a **Unit 7**, **Unit 9**, and **Unit 10** together as shown to make **Unit 11**. Make 2 **Unit 11's**.

Unit 11
(make 2)

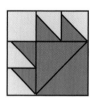

10. Sew a cream rectangle (C) and a **Unit 3** together as shown to make **Unit 12**. Make 2 **Unit 12's**.

Unit 12
(make 2)

11. Sew a cream rectangle (C), a **Unit 5**, and a cream square (B) together as shown to make **Unit 13**. Make 2 **Unit 13's**.

Unit 13
(make 2)

12. Sew a **Unit 11**, **Unit 12**, and **Unit 13** together as shown to make **Block B1**. Make 2 **Block B1's**.

Block B1 Diagram
(make 2)

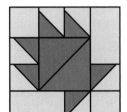

13. Repeat Block B, Steps 7 - 12 using **Unit 4's**, **Unit 6's**, **Unit 8's**, cream rectangles (C), and cream squares (B) to make 2 **Block B2's**.

Block B2 Diagram
(make 2)

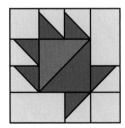

14. Follow **Quilting Instructions**, page 90, to layer backing square (J), fleece square (S), and **Block B** together. Quilt "in-the-ditch" along each seam.

Corner Setting Triangle
1. Follow **Quilting Instructions**, page 90, to mark blue plaid triangle (M) using **Template 1**, page 37.
2. Layer blue plaid triangle (N), fleece triangle (U), and blue plaid triangle (M) together. Quilt using a contrasting color thread to make **Corner Setting Triangle**. Make 4 **Corner Setting Triangles**.

Corner Setting Triangle
(make 4)

Side Setting Triangle
1. Follow **Quilting Instructions**, page 90, to mark blue plaid triangle (K) using **Template 2**, page 37.
2. Layer blue plaid triangle (L), fleece triangle (T), and blue plaid triangle (K) together. Quilt using a contrasting color thread to make **Side Setting Triangle**. Make 4 **Side Setting Triangles**.

Side Setting Triangle
(make 4)

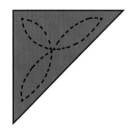

ASSEMBLING THE QUILT

As the quilt is assembled, the rag seams are created on the front of the quilt by sewing the blocks and borders together with back sides together. Refer to **Assembling The Quilt***, page 88, for additional information. Use ¹/₂" seam allowance to assemble quilt.*

1. Sew 2 **Corner Setting Triangles**, 2 **Block B1's**, and **Block A** together to make **Unit 14**.

Unit 14

2. Sew 1 **Corner Setting Triangle**, **Block B2**, and 2 **Side Setting Triangles** together to make **Unit 15**. Referring to **Quilt Diagram** for placement of **Block B2**, make second **Unit 15**.

Unit 15

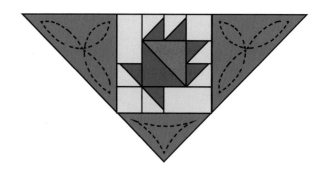

3. Sew 2 **Unit 15's** and **Unit 14** together.

COMPLETING THE QUILT

Refer to page 89 for Steps 1-3.

1. Make and attach a hanging sleeve (P) to back of quilt.
2. Sew trim strips (V) to edges of quilt.
3. Fringe rag seams. Wash and dry quilt.
4. Sew button to flower center.

Quilt Diagram

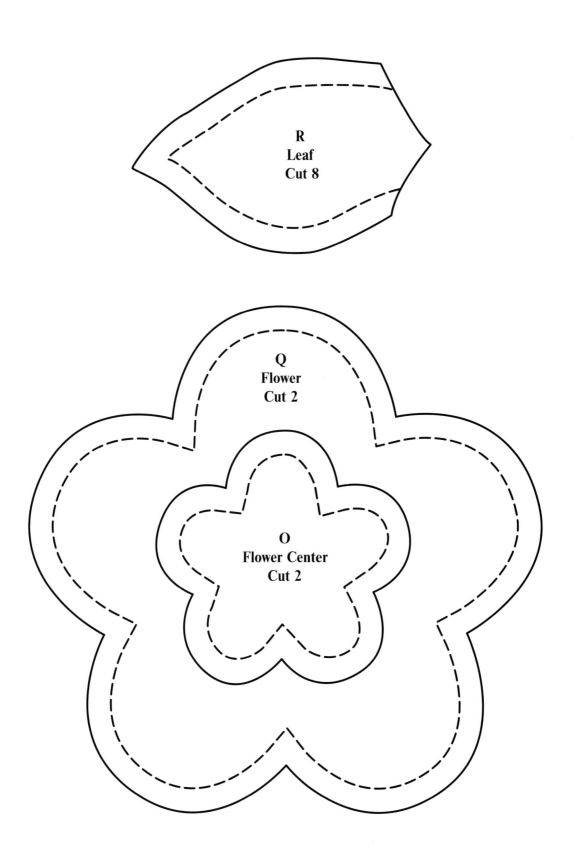

R
Leaf
Cut 8

Q
Flower
Cut 2

O
Flower Center
Cut 2

Template 1

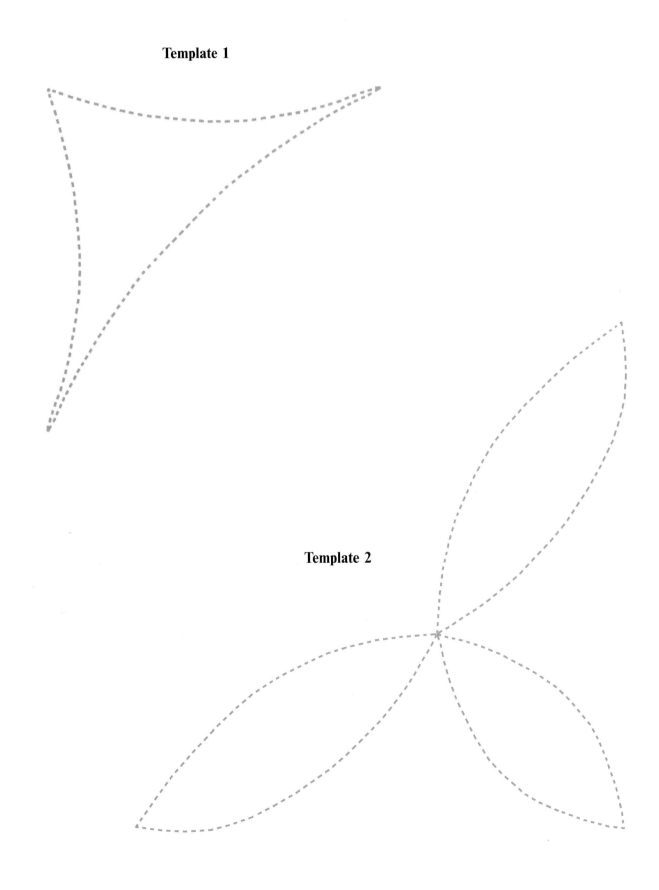

Template 2

June

Finished Block Size: $4^1/_2$" x $4^1/_2$" (11 cm x 11 cm)
Finished Size (including outer fringe): $23^1/_2$" x $23^1/_2$" (60 cm x 60 cm)

$^1/_2$ yd (46 cm) of beige plaid

$^1/_2$ yd (46 cm) of blue plaid

$^1/_2$ yd (46 cm) of pink plaid

$^3/_4$ yd (69 cm) of green plaid

$^1/_4$ yd (23 cm) of trim fabric

$^3/_8$ yd (34 cm) of fleece for batting

CUTTING OUT THE BLOCKS

*Refer to **Rotary Cutting**, page 84, before beginning project.*

From beige plaid:
- Cut 1 strip $5^1/_2$" wide. From this strip, cut 5 squares (A) $5^1/_2$" x $5^1/_2$" for Block A.
- Cut 2 strips $5^7/_8$" wide. From these strips, cut 8 squares (B) $5^7/_8$" x $5^7/_8$" for Blocks C, D, and E.

From blue plaid:
- Cut 2 strips $5^1/_2$" wide. From these strips, cut 4 squares (C) $5^1/_2$" x $5^1/_2$" for Block B and 4 squares (D) $5^1/_2$" x $5^1/_2$" for backings.
- Cut 1 strip $5^7/_8$" wide. From this strip, cut 2 squares (E) $5^7/_8$" x $5^7/_8$" for Block C.

From pink plaid:
- Cut 1 strip $5^7/_8$" wide. From this strip, cut 4 squares (F) $5^7/_8$" x $5^7/_8$" for Block D.
- Cut 2 strips $5^1/_2$" wide. From these strips, cut 8 squares (G) $5^1/_2$" x $5^1/_2$" for Block D backings.

From green plaid:
- Cut 1 strip $5^7/_8$" wide. From this strip, cut 2 squares (H) $5^7/_8$" x $5^7/_8$" for Block E.
- Cut 2 strips $5^1/_2$" wide. From these strips, cut 13 squares (I) $5^1/_2$" x $5^1/_2$" for Blocks A, C, and E backings.
- Cut 1 rectangle (J) $21^1/_2$" x 8" for hanging sleeve.

From fleece:
- Cut 3 strips $4^1/_4$" wide. From these strips, cut 25 squares (K) $4^1/_4$" x $4^1/_4$".

From trim fabric:
- Cut 4 strips (L) $1^1/_2$" x 24".

MAKING THE BLOCKS

*Each Block is pieced and quilted before the quilt is assembled. Follow **Piecing and Pressing**, page 87, to make blocks. **Note:** Use $^1/_4$" seam allowance to piece together blocks.*

Block A

1. Follow **Quilting Instructions**, page 90, to layer green plaid backing square (I), fleece square (K), and beige plaid square (A) together. Quilt each square with an X as shown to complete **Block A**. Make 5 **Block A's**.

Block A Diagram
(make 5)

Block B

1. Follow **Quilting Instructions**, page 90, to mark blue plaid square (C) using **Template 1**, page 41.
2. Layer blue plaid backing square (D), fleece square (K), and blue plaid square (C) together. Quilt marked design to make **Block B**. Make 4 **Block B's**.

Block B Diagram
(make 4)

Block C

1. Draw a diagonal line (corner to corner) on wrong side of each beige plaid square (B). With right sides together, place a beige plaid square (B) on top of a blue plaid square (E). Stitch seam ¹/₄" from each side of drawn line (**Fig. 1**).

Fig. 1

2. Trim along drawn line and press open to make 2 **Block C** triangle-squares. Make 4 **Block C's**.

Block C Diagram
(make 4)

3. Follow **Quilting Instructions**, page 90, to mark blue plaid triangle using **Template 2**, page 41.

4. Layer green plaid backing square (I), fleece square (K), and **Block C** together. Quilt blue plaid triangle as marked, beige plaid triangle with a diagonal line, and "in the ditch" along the seam (**Fig. 2**).

Fig. 2

Block D

1. Refer to **Block C**, Steps 1 - 3, to make 8 **Block D's** using beige plaid square (B), pink plaid square (F), pink plaid backing square (G), and fleece square (K).

Block D Diagram
(make 8)

Block E

1. Refer to **Block C**, Steps 1 - 3, to make 4 **Block E's** using beige plaid square (B), green plaid square (H), green plaid backing square (I), and fleece square (K).

Block E Diagram
(make 4)

ASSEMBLING THE QUILT

*Refer to **General Instructions**, page 81, to make the quilt. Refer to **Quilt Diagram** and photo, page 38, for placement. Use ¹/₂" seam allowance to assemble quilt.*

1. Sew 2 **Block E's**, 2 **Block D's**, and **Block A** together to make **Unit 1**. Make 2 **Unit 1's**.

Unit 1
(make 2)

2. Sew 2 **Block D's**, 2 **Block C's**, and **Block B** together to make **Unit 2**. Make 2 **Unit 2's**.

Unit 2
(make 2)

3. Sew 2 **Block B's** and 3 **Block A's** together to make **Unit 3**.

Unit 3

4. Sew 2 **Unit 1's**, 2 **Unit 2's**, and **Unit 3** together to make quilt.

COMPLETING THE QUILT

Refer to page 89 for Steps 1-3.

1. Make and attach a hanging sleeve (J) to back of quilt.

2. Sew trim strips (L) to edges of quilt.

3. Fringe rag seams. Wash and dry quilt.

Quilt Diagram

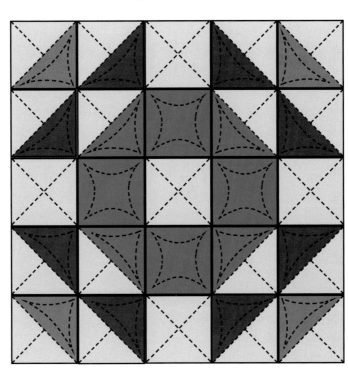

Template 1

Template 2

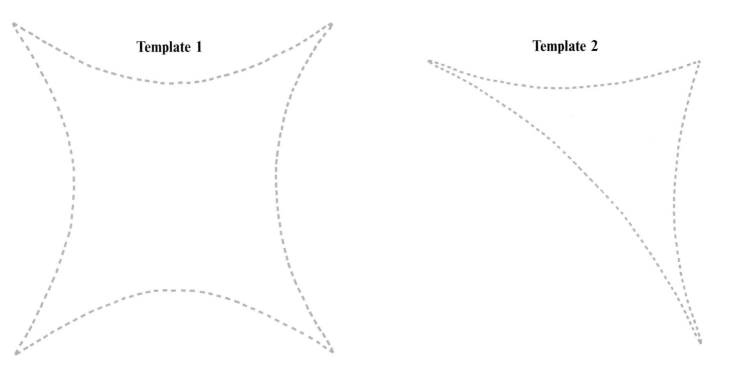

July

Finished Block Size: 4" x 4" (10 cm x 10 cm)
Finished Size (including outer fringe): 33" x 25" (84 cm x 64 cm)

Yardage is based on 45"w fabric.

$^3/_8$ yd (34 cm) of beige solid
$^1/_8$ yd (11 cm) of beige plaid No. 1
$^1/_4$ yd (23 cm) of beige plaid No. 2
$1^1/_4$ yds (1.1 m) of beige plaid No. 3
$^1/_8$ yd (11 cm) **each** of red plaids No. 1 and 2
$^1/_4$ yd (23 cm) **each** of red plaids No. 3-8
$^1/_4$ yd (23 cm) of blue plaid No. 1

$^1/_8$ yd (11 cm) **each** of blue plaids No. 2-9
$^5/_8$ yd (57 cm) of fleece for batting
$^1/_4$ yd (23 cm) of trim fabric
You will also need:
Paper-backed fusible web
Stabilizer

CUTTING OUT THE BLOCKS

Refer to **Rotary Cutting**, *page 84, before beginning project.*

From beige solid:
- Refer to **Satin Stitch Appliqué**, page 91, to use pattern, page 47, to cut 1 star (A).
- Cut 3 strips $3^1/_4$" wide. From these strips, cut 26 squares (B) $3^1/_4$" x $3^1/_4$" for Blocks B1, B2, B3, and B4.

From beige plaid No. 1:
- Cut 1 strip $3^1/_4$" wide. From this strip, cut 10 squares (C) $3^1/_4$" x $3^1/_4$" for Blocks B1 and B5.

From beige plaid No. 2:
- Cut 2 strips $3^1/_4$" wide. From these strips, cut 13 squares (D) $3^1/_4$" x $3^1/_4$" for Blocks B2 and B3.

From beige plaid No. 3:
- Cut 2 strips $3^1/_4$" wide. From these strips, cut 16 squares (E) $3^1/_4$" x $3^1/_4$" for Blocks B4 and B6.
- Cut 5 strips 5" wide. From these strips, cut 39 squares (F) 5" x 5" for backings.
- Cut 1 rectangle (G) 31" x 8" for hanging sleeve.

From red plaid No. 1:
- Cut 1 strip $3^1/_4$" wide. From this strip, cut 5 squares (H) $3^1/_4$" x $3^1/_4$" for Block B5.

From red plaid No. 2:
- Cut 1 strip $3^1/_4$" wide. From this strip, cut 8 squares (I) $3^1/_4$" x $3^1/_4$" for Block B6.

From *each* red plaid No. 3, 4, and 5:
- Cut 1 strip 5" wide. From this strip, cut 5 squares (J, K, and L) 5" x 5" for Blocks B5, B1, and B2.

From *each* red plaid No. 6, 7, and 8:
- Cut 1 strip 5" wide. From this strip, cut 8 squares (M, N, and O) 5" x 5" for Blocks B3, B4, and B6.

From blue plaid No. 1:
- Cut 1 strip 5" wide. From this strip, cut 1 background square (P) 5" x 5" for Block A center and 1 square (Q) 5" x 5" for Block A center backing.

From blue plaid No. 2:
- Cut 1 strip 3" wide. From this strip, cut 1 rectangle (R) 5" x 3" for Block A and 1 rectangle (S) 5" x 3 for backing.

From *each* blue plaid No. 3 and 4:
- Cut 1 strip 3" wide. From this strip, cut 1 rectangle (T and U) 7" x 3" for Block A and 1 rectangle (V and W) 7" x 3" for backing.

From *each* blue plaid No. 5 and 6:
- Cut 1 strip 3" wide. From this strip, cut 1 rectangle (X and Y) 9" x 3" for Block A and 1 rectangle (Z and a) 9" x 3" for backing.

From *each* blue plaid No. 7 and 8:
- Cut 1 strip 3" wide. From this strip, cut 1 rectangle (b and c) 11" x 3" for Block A and 1 rectangle (d and e) 11" x 3" for backing.

From blue plaid No. 9:
- Cut 1 strip 3" wide. From this strip, cut 1 rectangle (f) 13" x 3" for Block A and 1 rectangle (g) 13" x 3" for backing.

From fleece:
- Cut 4 strips $3^3/_4$" wide. From these strips, cut 40 squares (h) $3^3/_4$" x $3^3/_4$" for Block A center and Blocks B1 - B6.
- Cut 2 strips $1^3/_4$" wide. From these strips, cut 1 rectangle (i) $3^3/_4$" x $1^3/_4$", 2 rectangles (j) $5^3/_4$" x $1^3/_4$", 2 rectangles (k) $7^3/_4$" x $1^3/_4$", 2 rectangles (l) $9^3/_4$" x $1^3/_4$", and 1 rectangle (m) $11^3/_4$" x $1^3/_4$" for Block A.

From trim fabric:
- Cut 2 strips (n) 34" x $1^1/_2$".
- Cut 2 strips (o) $1^1/_2$" x 26".

MAKING THE BLOCKS

*Each Block is pieced and quilted before the quilt is assembled. Follow **Piecing and Pressing**, page 87, to make blocks. **Note:** Use ¹/₄" seam allowance to piece together blocks.*

Block A

1. Fuse star appliqué to No. 1 blue plaid background square (P) to make **Unit 1**.

Unit 1

2. Follow **Quilting Instructions**, page 90, to layer backing square (Q), fleece square (h), and **Unit 1** together.

3. Follow **Satin Stitch Appliqué**, page 91, to appliqué star in place through all layers to make block center.

4. Follow **Quilting Instructions**, page 90, to layer blue plaid rectangles (R, T, U, X, Y, b, c, and f), blue plaid backing rectangles (S, V, W, Z, a, d, e, and g), and fleece rectangles (i - m) together to make **Units 2 - 9**. Quilt with a straight line down the center of each rectangle (**Fig. 1**).

Fig. 1

5. Follow **Assembling the Quilt**, page 88, and **Block A Diagram** to sew **Units 1 - 9** together in numerical order to make **Block A**.

Block A Diagram

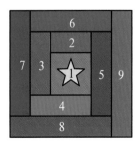

Block B1

1. Draw a diagonal line (corner to corner) on wrong side of each beige plaid square (B, C, D, and E). With right sides together and matching raw edges, place a beige plaid square on top of a red plaid square (K, L, M, or N). Stitch seam on drawn line (**Fig. 2**). Trim seam allowance to ¹/₄"; press.

Fig. 2

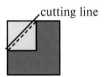

cutting line

2. Repeat Step 1 to sew a different beige plaid square to the opposite corner to make **Blocks B1 - B4**. Make 5 **Block B1's** and **B2's**. Make 8 **Block B3's** and **B4's**.

Block B1 Diagram
(make 5)

Block B2 Diagram
(make 5)

Block B3 Diagram
(make 8)

Block B4 Diagram

(make 8)

3. Repeat Steps 1 and 2 using 1 red plaid square (H or I), 1 beige plaid square (C or E), and 1 red plaid square (J or O) to make **Blocks B5** and **B6**. Make 5 **Block B5's** and 8 **Block B6's**.

Block B5 Diagram

(make 5)

Block B6 Diagram

(make 8)

4. Follow **Quilting Instructions**, page 90, to layer beige plaid backing squares (F), fleece squares (h), and **Blocks B1 - B6** together. Quilt "in the ditch" and diagonally as shown in **Fig. 3**.

Fig. 3

ASSEMBLING THE QUILT

As the quilt is assembled, the rag seams are created on the front of the quilt by sewing the blocks and borders together with back sides together. Refer to **Assembling The Quilt**, *page 88, for additional information. Use* **¹/₂" seam allowance** *to assemble quilt.*

1. Sew 5 **Block B5's** together as shown to make **Unit 10**.

Unit 10

2. Sew 5 **Block B1's** together as shown to make **Unit 11**.

Unit 11

3. Sew 5 **Block B2's** together as shown to make **Unit 12**.

Unit 12

4. Sew 8 **Block B3's** together as shown to make **Unit 13**.

Unit 13

5. Sew 8 **Block B4's** together as shown to make **Unit 14**.

Unit 14

6. Sew 8 **Block B6's** together as shown to make **Unit 15**.

Unit 15

7. Sew **Units 10**, **11**, and **12** together as shown to make **Unit 16**.

Unit 16

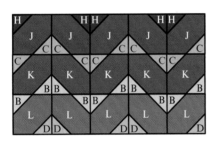

8. Sew **Block A** and **Unit 16** together as shown to make **Unit 17**.

Unit 17

9. Sew **Units 13**, **14**, **15**, and **17** together as shown.

COMPLETING THE QUILT
Refer to page 89 for Steps 1-3.

1. Using rectangle (G), make and attach a hanging sleeve to back of quilt.
2. Sew trim strips (n) to top and bottom edges of quilt. Sew trim strips (o) to side edges of quilt.
3. Fringe rag seams. Wash and dry quilt.

Quilt Diagram

Unit 17

Unit 13

Unit 14

Unit 15

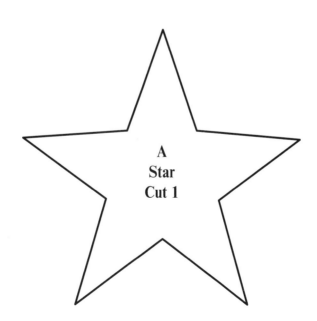

A
Star
Cut 1

August

Finished Block Size: $5^3/4$" x $5^3/4$" (15 cm x 15 cm)
Finished Size (including outer fringe): $23^1/4$" x $23^1/4$" (59 cm x 59 cm)

$^3/_8$ yd (34 cm) of cream fabric
Scrap of blue print for block center
$^1/_2$ yd (46 cm) of blue plaid No. 1
$^3/_4$ yd (69 cm) of blue plaid No. 2

$^1/_8$ yd (11 cm) of blue plaid No. 3
$^3/_8$ yd (34 cm) of blue plaid No. 4
$^1/_2$ yd (46 cm) of fleece for batting
$^1/_4$ yd (23 cm) of trim fabric

CUTTING OUT THE BLOCKS AND BORDERS

Refer to **Rotary Cutting**, *page 84, before beginning project.*

From cream fabric:
- Cut 2 strips $2^3/_4$" wide. From these strips, cut 16 squares (A) $2^3/_4$" x $2^3/_4$" for Block A.
- Cut 1 strip $3^3/_8$" wide. From this strip, cut 8 squares (B) $3^3/_8$" x $3^3/_8$" for Block A.

From blue print:
- Cut 4 squares (C) $2^1/_4$" x $2^1/_4$" for Block A center.

From blue plaid No. 1:
- Cut 1 strip $3^3/_8$" wide. From this strip, cut 8 squares (D) $3^3/_8$" x $3^3/_8$" for Block A.
- Cut 1 strip $6^3/_4$" wide. From this strip, cut 4 squares (E) $6^3/_4$" x $6^3/_4$" for Block A backings.
- Cut 1 strip $4^1/_2$" wide. From this strip, cut 4 squares (F) $3^1/_2$" x $3^1/_2$" for Block C and 4 squares (G) $3^1/_2$" x $3^1/_2$" for Block C backings.

From blue plaid No. 2:
- Cut 2 strips $6^3/_4$" wide. From these strips, cut 5 squares (H) $6^3/_4$" x $6^3/_4$" for Block B and 5 squares (I) $6^3/_4$" x $6^3/_4$" for Block B backings.
- Cut 1 rectangle (J) $21^1/_4$" x 8" for hanging sleeve.

From blue plaid No. 3:
- Cut 2 strips 2" wide. From these strips, cut 4 rectangles (K) $18^1/_4$" x 2" for Block D.

From blue plaid No. 4:
- Cut 2 strips 2" wide. From these strips, cut 4 rectangles (L) $18^1/_4$" x 2" for Block D.
- Cut 2 strips $3^1/_2$" wide. From these strips, cut 4 rectangles (M) $18^1/_4$" x $3^1/_2$" for Block D backings.

From fleece:
- Cut 2 strips $5^1/_2$" wide. From these strips, cut 9 squares (N) $5^1/_2$" x $5^1/_2$" for Blocks A and B.
- Cut 2 strips $2^1/_4$" wide. From these strips, cut 4 squares (O) $2^1/_4$" x $2^1/_4$" for Block C and 4 rectangles (P) 17" x $2^1/_4$" for Block D.

From trim fabric:
- Cut 4 strips (Q) $1^1/_2$" x 24".

MAKING THE BLOCKS AND BORDERS

*Each Block and Border is pieced and quilted before the quilt is assembled. Follow **Piecing and Pressing**, page 87, to make blocks. **Note:** Use ¹/₄" seam allowance to piece together blocks and border strips.*

Block A

1. Draw a diagonal line (corner to corner) on wrong side of each cream square (B). With right sides together, place a cream square (B) on top of a No. 1 blue plaid square (D). Stitch seam ¹/₄" from each side of drawn line (**Fig. 1**).

Fig. 1

2. Cut along drawn line and press open to make 2 triangle-squares. Trim ¹/₈" from the cream sides and bottom blue side and ⁵/₈" from the right blue side of each triangle-square (**Fig. 2**) to make a **Unit 1** rectangle (2¹/₄" x 2³/₄"). Make 16 **Unit 1's.**

Fig. 2

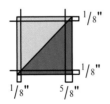

Unit 1
(make 16)

3. Sew 2 cream squares (A) and a **Unit 1** together as shown to make **Unit 2**. Make 8 **Unit 2's.**

Unit 2
(make 8)

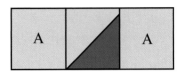

4. Sew 2 **Unit 1's** and a blue print square (C) together as shown to make **Unit 3**. Make 4 **Unit 3's.**

Unit 3
(make 4)

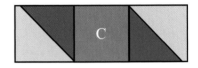

5. Sew 2 **Unit 2's** and a **Unit 3** together as shown to make **Block A**. Make 4 **Block A's.**

Block A Diagram
(make 4)

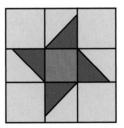

6. Follow **Quilting Instructions**, page 90, to layer backing square (E), fleece square (N), and **Block A** together. Quilt "in-the-ditch" along each seam to complete the block.

Block B

1. Follow **Quilting Instructions**, page 90, to mark No. 2 blue plaid square (H) using **Template 1**, page 53.
2. Layer No. 2 blue plaid backing square (I), fleece square (N), and No. 2 blue plaid square (H) together. Quilt marked design to make **Block B**. Make 5 **Block B's.**

Block B Diagram
(make 5)

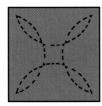

Block C

1. Follow **Quilting Instructions**, page 90, to layer No. 1 blue plaid backing square (G), fleece square (O), and No. 1 blue plaid corner square (F) together.
2. Quilt corner square with an X to make **Block C**. Make 4 **Block C's**.

Block C Diagram
(make 4)

Block D

1. Matching right sides and long edges, sew a No. 3 blue plaid rectangle (K) and a No. 4 blue plaid rectangle (L) together to make **Unit 4**. Make 4 **Unit 4's**.

Unit 4
(make 4)

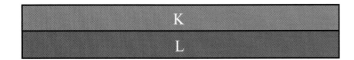

2. Follow **Quilting Instructions**, page 90, to mark **Unit 4** using **Template 2**, page 53.
3. Layer No. 4 blue plaid backing rectangle (M), fleece rectangle (P), and **Unit 4** together. Quilt marked design to make **Block D**. Make 4 **Block D's**.

Block D Diagram
(make 4)

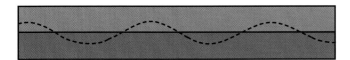

ASSEMBLING THE QUILT

As the quilt is assembled, the rag seams are created on the front of the quilt by sewing the blocks and borders together with back sides together. Refer to **Assembling The Quilt**, *page 88, for additional information. Use $^1/_2"$ seam allowance to assemble quilt.*

1. Sew 2 **Block B's** and 1 **Block A** together as shown to make **Unit 5**. Make 2 **Unit 5's**.

Unit 5
(make 2)

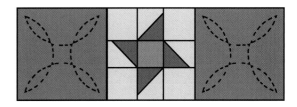

2. Sew 2 **Block A's** and 1 **Block B** together as shown to make **Unit 6**.

Unit 6

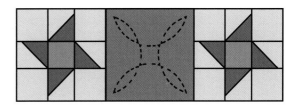

3. Sew 2 **Unit 5's** and a **Unit 6** together to make quilt center.
4. Sew a **Block D** to each side of quilt center.
5. Sew a **Block C** to each end of **Block D** to make **Unit 7**. Make 2 **Unit 7's**.

Unit 7
(make 2)

6. Sew a **Unit 7** to the top and bottom of quilt center.

COMPLETING THE QUILT

Refer to page 89 for Steps 1-3.

1. Make and attach a hanging sleeve (J) to back of quilt.

2. Sew trim strips (Q) to edges of quilt.

3. Fringe rag seams. Wash and dry quilt.

Quilt Diagram

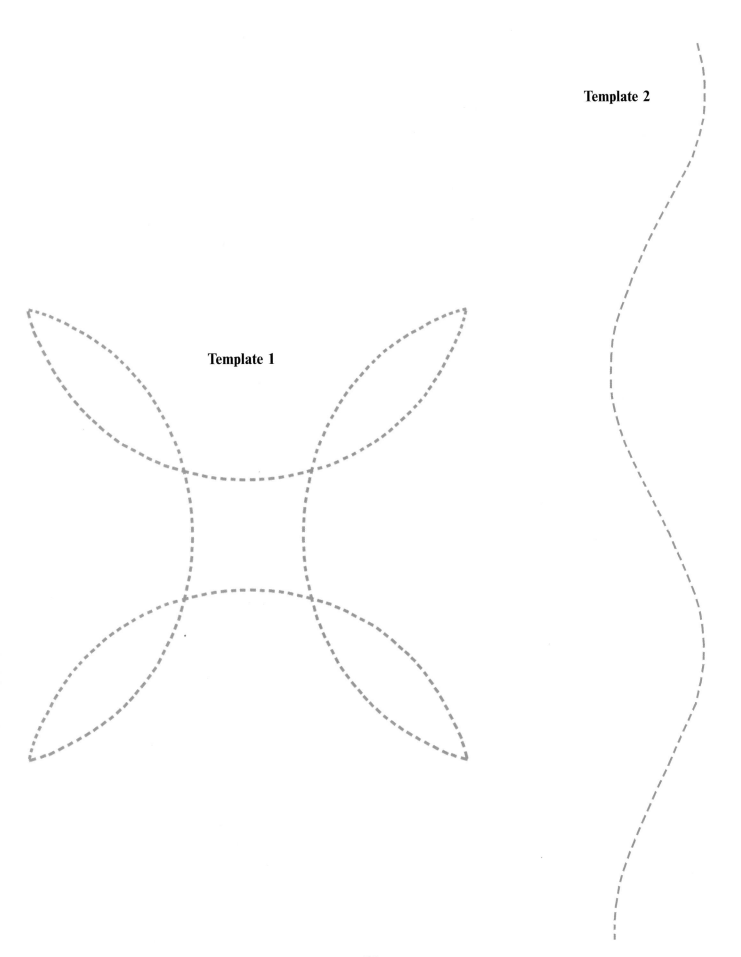

Template 1

Template 2

September

Finished Block Size: 5³/₄" x 5³/₄" (15 cm x 15 cm)
Finished Size (including outer fringe): 24¹/₄" x 24¹/₄" (62 cm x 62 cm)

$^1/_8$ yd (11 cm) of red print
$^3/_8$ yd (34 cm) of dark green check
$^3/_8$ yd (34 cm) of beige plaid
$^1/_8$ yd (11 cm) **each** of 4 assorted green plaids
$^1/_8$ yd (11 cm) **each** of 4 assorted
   red/green plaids
$^5/_8$ yd (57 cm) of red/green plaid No. 1

$^3/_8$ yd (34 cm) of red/green plaid No. 2
$^1/_2$ yd (46 cm) of fleece for batting
$^1/_4$ yd (23 cm) of trim fabric
You will also need:
   Paper-backed fusible web
   Stabilizer

CUTTING OUT THE BLOCKS AND BORDERS

*Refer to **Rotary Cutting**, page 84, and **Satin Stitch Appliqué**, page 91, before beginning project.*

From red print:
- Use pattern, page 59, to cut 4 apples (A) for Block A.

From dark green check:
- Use patterns, page 59, to cut 4 leaves (B) and 4 leaves (C) for Block A.
- Cut 1 strip $6^3/_4$" wide. From this strip, cut 4 squares (D) $6^3/_4$" x $6^3/_4$" for Block A backings.
- Cut 1 strip 4" wide. From this strip, cut 4 squares (E) 4" x 4" for Block C backings.

From beige plaid:
- Cut 1 strip $6^3/_4$" wide. From this strip, cut 4 background squares (F) $6^3/_4$" x $6^3/_4$" for Block A.
- Cut 2 strips $2^1/_4$" wide. From these strips, cut 20 rectangles (G) $2^1/_4$" x $2^3/_4$" for Block B.

From *each* of 4 assorted green plaids:
- Cut 1 strip 3" wide. From this strip, cut 4 squares (H1, H2, H3, and H4) 3" x 3" for Block A.

From red/green plaid No. 1:
- Cut 4 strips 4" wide. From these strips, cut 4 rectangles (I) $18^1/_4$" x 4" for Block D and 4 rectangles (J) $18^1/_4$" x 4" for Block D backings.
- Cut 1 strip $2^1/_4$" wide. From this strip, cut 5 squares (K) $2^1/_4$" x $2^1/_4$" for Block B centers.

From red/green plaid No. 2:
- Cut 1 strip $6^3/_4$" wide. From this strip, cut 5 squares (L) $6^3/_4$" x $6^3/_4$" for Block B backings.
- Cut 1 strip $3^1/_2$" wide. From this strip, cut 4 rectangles (M) $3^1/_2$" x 6" for hanging tabs.

From *each* of 4 assorted red/green plaids:
- Cut 1 strip $2^3/_4$" wide. From this strip, cut 5 squares (N1, N2, N3, and N4) $2^3/_4$" x $2^3/_4$" for Block B.

From fleece:
- Cut 2 strips $5^1/_2$" wide. From these strips, cut 9 squares (O) $5^1/_2$" x $5^1/_2$" for Blocks A and B.
- Cut 2 strips $2^3/_4$" wide. From these strips, cut 4 squares (P) $2^3/_4$" x $2^3/_4$" for Block C and 4 rectangles (Q) 17" x $2^3/_4$" for Block D.

From trim fabric:
- Cut 4 strips (R) $1^1/_2$" x 25".

MAKING THE BLOCKS AND BORDERS

*Each Block and Border is pieced and quilted before the quilt is assembled. Follow **Piecing and Pressing**, page 87, to make blocks. **Note: Use ¹/₄" seam allowance** to piece together blocks and border strips.*

Block A

1. Draw a diagonal line (corner to corner) on wrong side of each green plaid square (H1, H2, H3, and H4). With right sides together and matching raw edges, place a green plaid square (H1) on top of a beige plaid background square (F). Stitch seam on drawn line; stitch again ¹/₂" from seam (**Fig. 1**). Cut halfway between seams, making a **Unit 1** triangle-square that will be used for **Block C**. Press seam.

Fig. 1

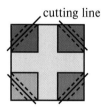

cutting line

Unit 1
(make 16)

2. Sew remaining green plaid squares (H2, H3, and H4) to beige plaid background square (F) to make **Unit 2**. Make 4 **Unit 2's**.

Unit 2
(make 4)

3. Refer to **Satin Stitch Appliqué**, page 91, to fuse apple (A) and leaf (B and C) appliqués to **Unit 2**.

4. Follow **Quilting Instructions**, page 90, to layer dark green check backing square (D), fleece square (O), and **Unit 2** together. Quilt "in the ditch" along each seam.

5. Follow **Satin Stitch Appliqué**, page 91, to appliqué apple and leaves in place through all layers to make **Block A**. Make 4 **Block A's**.

Block A Diagram
(make 4)

Block B

1. Sew a beige plaid rectangle (G) and 2 red/green plaid squares (N1 and N2) together as shown to make **Unit 3**. Make 5 **Unit 3's**.

Unit 3
(make 5)

2. Sew 2 beige plaid rectangles (G) and a No. 1 red/green plaid square (K) together as shown to make **Unit 4**. Make 5 **Unit 4's**.

Unit 4
(make 5)

3. Sew a beige plaid rectangle (G) and 2 red/green plaid squares (N3 and N4) together as shown to make **Unit 5**. Make 5 **Unit 5's**.

Unit 5
(make 5)

4. Sew **Units 3**, **4**, and **5** together to make **Block B**. Make 5 **Block B's**.

Block B Diagram
(make 5)

5. Follow **Quilting Instructions**, page 90, to layer No. 2 red/green plaid backing square (L), fleece square (O), and **Block B** together. Quilt "in the ditch" along each seam to complete the block.

Block C
1. Sew 2 different **Unit 1** triangle-squares together as shown to make **Unit 6**. Make 4 **Unit 6's**.

Unit 6
(make 4)

2. Sew 2 **Unit 6's** together as shown to make **Block C1**. Make 2 **Block C1's**.

Block C1 Diagram
(make 2)

3. Sew 2 different **Unit 1** triangle-squares together as shown to make **Unit 7**. Make 4 **Unit 7's**.

Unit 7
(make 4)

4. Sew 2 **Unit 7's** together as shown to make **Block C2**. Make 2 **Block C2's**.

Block C2 Diagram
(make 2)

5. Follow **Quilting Instructions**, page 90, to layer backing squares (E), fleece squares (P), and **Blocks C1** and **C2** together.

6. Quilt each block "in-the-ditch" along each seam.

Block D
1. Follow **Quilting Instructions**, page 90, to mark No. 1 red/green plaid rectangle (I) using **Template**, page 59.

2. Layer No. 1 red/green plaid backing rectangle (J), fleece rectangle (Q), and No. 1 red/green plaid rectangle (I) together. Quilt marked design to make **Block D**. Make 4 **Block D's**.

Block D Diagram
(make 4)

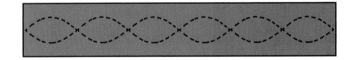

ASSEMBLING THE QUILT
As the quilt is assembled, the rag seams are created on the front of the quilt by sewing the blocks and borders together with back sides together. Refer to Assembling The Quilt, page 88, for additional information. Use $^1/_2$" seam allowance to assemble quilt.

1. Sew a **Block A** and 2 **Block B's** together as shown to make **Unit 8**. Make 2 **Unit 8's**.

Unit 8
(make 2)

2. Sew a **Block B** and 2 **Block A's** together as shown to make **Unit 9**.

Unit 9

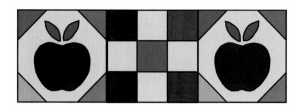

3. Sew 2 **Unit 8's** and a **Unit 9** together to make quilt center.
4. Sew a **Block D** to each side of quilt center.

5. Sew a **Block C1** to the left end and a **Block C2** to the right end of a **Block D** to make **Unit 10**. Make 2 **Unit 10's**.

Unit 10
(make 2)

6. Sew a **Unit 10** to the top and bottom of quilt center.

COMPLETING THE QUILT
Refer to page 89 for Steps 1-3.
1. Using No. 2 red/green plaid rectangles (M), make and attach 4 hanging tabs to back of quilt.
2. Sew trim strips (R) to edges of quilt.
3. Fringe rag seams. Wash and dry quilt.

Quilt Diagram

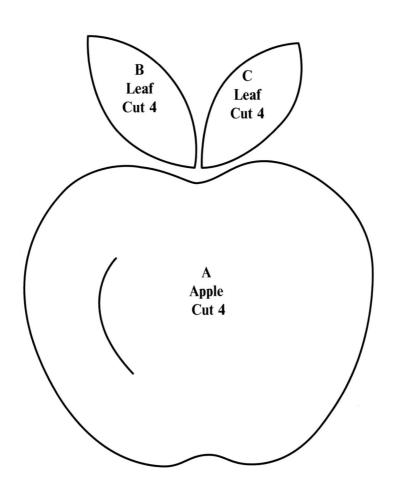

B
Leaf
Cut 4

C
Leaf
Cut 4

A
Apple
Cut 4

Template

October

Finished Block Size: 5" x 5" (13 cm x 13 cm)
Finished Size (including outer fringe): 22" x 22" (56 cm x 56 cm)

Yardage is based on 45"w fabric.

⅝ yd (57 cm) of beige plaid
⅜ yd (34 cm) of dark green plaid
¾ yd (69 cm) of rust plaid No. 1
Scrap of rust plaid No. 2
Scrap of brown plaid
¼ yd (23 cm) of orange plaid

¼ yd (23 cm) **each** of 5 assorted
orange and rust plaids
¼ yd (23 cm) of trim fabric
⅜ yd (34 cm) of fleece for batting
You will also need:
Paper-backed fusible web

CUTTING OUT THE BLOCKS AND BORDERS

*Refer to **Rotary Cutting**, page 84, and **Frayed-Edge Appliqué**, page 91, before beginning project.*

From beige plaid:
- Cut 2 strips 6" wide. From these strips, cut 5 squares (A) 6" x 6" for Blocks A and C and 4 squares (B) 6" x 6" for Block C backings.
- Cut 1 square (C) 6¾" x 6¾" for Block B.

From dark green plaid:
- Cut 1 strip 3¾" wide. From this strip, cut 4 squares (D) 3¾" x 3¾" for Block A.
- Cut 1 square (E) 6" x 6" for Block A backing.
- Cut 1 square (F) 6¾" x 6¾" for Block B.

From rust plaid No. 1:
- Cut 1 strip 6⅜" wide. From this strip, cut 2 squares (G) 6⅜" x 6⅜" for Block B.
- Cut 1 strip 6" wide. From this strip, cut 4 squares (H) 6" x 6" for Block B backings.
- Cut 1 strip 4" wide. From this strip, cut 4 squares (I) 4" x 4" for Block D and 4 squares (J) 4" x 4" for Block D backings.
- Cut 1 rectangle (K) 20" x 8" for hanging sleeve.

From rust plaid No. 2:
- Use pattern, page 65, to cut 2 acorns on the bias (L).

From brown plaid:
- Use pattern, page 65, to cut 2 acorn tops on the bias (M).
- Use pattern, page 65, to cut 4 stems (N); cut 4 stems in reverse.

From orange plaid:
- Use pattern, page 65, to cut 8 pumpkins on the bias (O).

From each of 5 assorted rust and orange plaids:
- Cut 1 strip 4" wide. From this strip, cut 4 squares (P) 4" x 4" for Block E and 4 squares (Q) 4" x 4" for Block E backings.

From fleece:
- Cut 1 strip 4¾" wide. From this strip, cut 9 squares (R) 4¾" x 4¾" for Blocks A, B, and C.
- Cut 2 strips 2¾" wide. From these strips, cut 24 squares (S) 2¾" x 2¾" for Blocks D and E.

From trim fabric:
- Cut 4 strips (T) 1½" x 23".

MAKING THE BLOCKS AND BORDERS

*Each Block and Border is pieced and quilted before the quilt is assembled. Follow **Piecing and Pressing**, page 87, to make blocks. **Note:** Use $^1/4"$ seam allowance to piece together blocks and border strips.*

Block A

1. Draw a diagonal line (corner to corner) on wrong side of each green plaid square (D). With right sides together, place a green plaid square (D) on top of a beige plaid square (A). Stitch seam on drawn line (**Fig. 1**).

Fig. 1

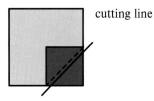

cutting line

2. Trim $^1/4"$ from drawn line and press open. Repeat for remaining 3 corners to make a **Unit 1** square.

Unit 1

3. Follow **Quilting Instructions**, page 90, to layer backing square (E), fleece square (R), and **Unit 1** together. Quilt "in-the-ditch" along each seam.

4. Using a $^3/16"$ seam allowance, follow **Frayed-Edge Appliqué**, page 91, to sew the acorn (L) and acorn top (M) to the center of **Unit 1** to make **Block A**.

Block A Diagram

Block B

1. Draw a diagonal line (corner to corner) on wrong side of beige plaid square (C). With right sides together, place a beige plaid square (C) on top of a green plaid square (F). Stitch seam $^1/4"$ from each side of drawn line (**Fig. 2**).

Fig. 2

2. Cut along drawn line and press open to make 2 **Unit 2** triangle-squares.

Unit 2
(make 2)

3. Draw a diagonal line (corner to corner) on wrong side of **Unit 2** triangle-squares. With right sides together, place a **Unit 2** triangle-square on top of a No. 1 rust plaid square (G). Stitch seam $^1/4"$ from each side of drawn line (**Fig. 3**).

Fig. 3

4. Cut along drawn line and press open to make **Block B1** and **Block B2**. Make 2 **Block B1's** and 2 **Block B2's**.

Block B1 Diagram
(make 2)

Block B2 Diagram
(make 2)

5. Follow **Quilting Instructions**, page 90, to layer backing squares (H), fleece squares (R), and **Blocks B1** and **B2** together. Quilt with an X as shown in **Fig. 4**.

Fig. 4

Block C

1. Follow **Quilting Instructions**, page 90, to mark pumpkin (O) and stem (N) and layer backing square (B), fleece square (R), and beige plaid square (A) together.

2. Using a ³/₁₆" seam allowance, sew the pumpkin and stem to the center of beige plaid square (A) to make **Block C**. Make 4 **Block C's**.

Block C Diagram
(make 4)

3. Refer to dotted lines on pattern to add quilting to pumpkin. Add tendrils using dark green thread and a triple stitch. See **Tip**, page 26.

Block D

1. Follow **Quilting Instructions**, page 90, to mark No. 1 rust plaid square (I) using **Template**, page 65. Layer backing square (J), fleece square (S), and No. 1 rust plaid square (I) together and quilt to make **Block D**. Make 4 **Block D's**.

Block D Diagram
(make 4)

Block E

1. Follow **Quilting Instructions**, page 90, to mark and layer backing square (Q), fleece square (S), and rust or orange square (P) together. Quilt with an X to make **Block E**. Make 20 **Block E's** (4 of each color).

Block E Diagram
(make 20)

ASSEMBLING THE QUILT

*As the quilt is assembled, the rag seams are created on the front of the quilt by sewing the blocks and borders together with back sides together. Refer to **Assembling The Quilt**, page 88, for additional information. Use ¹/₂" seam allowance to assemble quilt.*

1. Sew 2 **Block C's** and a **Block B2** together as shown to make **Unit 3**. Make 2 **Unit 3's**.

Unit 3
(make 2)

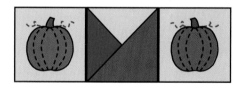

2. Sew 2 **Block B1's** and a **Block A** together as shown to make **Unit 4**.

Unit 4

3. Sew 2 **Unit 3's** and a **Unit 4** together as shown to make quilt center.
4. Sew 5 different **Block E's** together to make **Unit 5**. Make 2 **Unit 5's**.

Unit 5
(make 2)

5. Sew a **Unit 5** to each side of quilt center.
6. Sew 2 **Block D's** and 5 different **Block E's** together to make **Unit 6**. Make 2 **Unit 6's**.

Unit 6
(make 2)

7. Sew a **Unit 6** to the top and bottom of quilt center.

COMPLETING THE QUILT
Refer to page 89 for Steps 1-3.
1. Make and attach a hanging sleeve (K) to back of quilt.
2. Sew trim strips (T) to edges of quilt.
3. Fringe rag seams. Wash and dry quilt.

Quilt Diagram

64

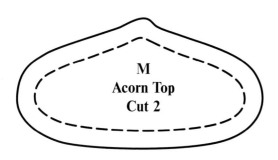

M
Acorn Top
Cut 2

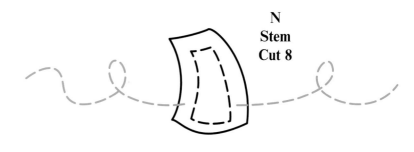

N
Stem
Cut 8

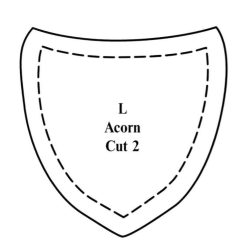

L
Acorn
Cut 2

Template

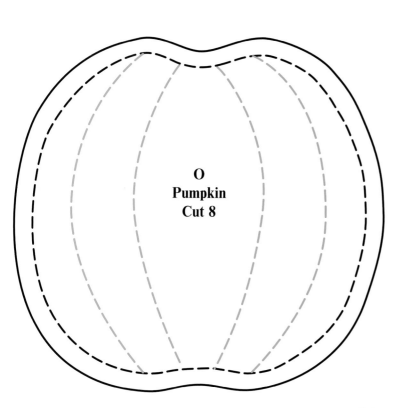

O
Pumpkin
Cut 8

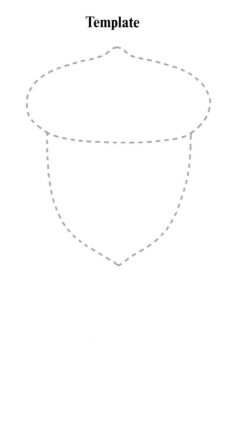

November

Finished Block Size: 6$\frac{1}{2}$" x 6$\frac{1}{2}$" (17 cm x 17 cm)
Finished Size (including outer fringe): 22" x 22" (56 cm x 56 cm)

$^5/_8$ yd (57 cm) of beige plaid

$^1/_4$ yd (23 cm) **each** of green, orange, rust, and gold plaids for leaf blocks

$^1/_4$ yd (23 cm) of rust plaid No. 1

$^1/_4$ yd (23 cm) of rust plaid No. 2

$^3/_8$ yd (34 cm) of dark green plaid No. 1

$^1/_2$ yd (46 cm) of dark green plaid No. 2

$^1/_2$ yd (46 cm) of fleece for batting

$^1/_4$ yd (23 cm) of trim fabric

CUTTING OUT THE BLOCKS

Refer to **Rotary Cutting**, *page 84, before beginning project.*

From beige plaid:

- Cut 1 strip 3" wide. From this strip, cut 4 squares (A) 3" x 3" for Block A.
- Cut 1 strip $3^1/_2$" wide. From this strip, cut 8 squares $3^1/_2$" x $3^1/_2$". Four squares (B) will be used for Units 2 and 3. Cut remaining 4 squares once diagonally to make 8 triangles (C) for Unit 4.
- Cut 1 strip 4" wide. From this strip, cut 4 squares (D) 4" x 4" for Unit 1.
- Cut 1 strip $7^1/_2$" wide. From this strip, cut 4 squares (E) $7^1/_2$" x $7^1/_2$" for Block A backings.

From each green, orange, rust, and gold plaid:

- Cut 1 strip $2^1/_2$" wide. From this strip, cut 1 square (F) $2^1/_2$" x $2^1/_2$" and 2 rectangles (G) $2^1/_2$" x 3" for Block A.
- Cut 1 square (H) 4" x 4" for Unit 1.
- Cut 1 square (I) $3^1/_2$" x $3^1/_2$" for Units 2 and 3.
- Cut 1 rectangle (J) 5" x 1" for Unit 4.

From rust plaid No. 1:

- Cut 2 strips 3" wide. From these strips, cut 2 rectangles (K) $7^1/_2$" x 3" for Block B1, 2 rectangles (L) $7^1/_2$" x 3" for Block B1 backings, 2 rectangles (M) $9^1/_2$" x 3" for Block C1, and 2 rectangles (N) $9^1/_2$" x 3" for Block C1 backings.

From rust plaid No. 2:

- Cut 2 strips 3" wide. From these strips, cut 2 rectangles (O) $7^1/_2$" x 3" for Block B2, 2 rectangles (P) $7^1/_2$" x 3" for Block B2 backings, 2 rectangles (Q) $9^1/_2$" x 3" for Block C2, and 2 rectangles (R) $9^1/_2$" x 3" for Block C2 backings.

From dark green plaid No. 1:

- Cut 3 strips 3" wide. From these strips, cut 2 rectangles (S) $9^1/_2$" x 3" for Block C3, 2 rectangles (T) $9^1/_2$" x 3" for Block C3 backings, 2 rectangles (U) $11^1/_2$" x 3" for Block D1, and 2 rectangles (V) $11^1/_2$" x 3" for Block D1 backings.

From dark green plaid No. 2:

- Cut 3 strips 3" wide. From these strips, cut 2 rectangles (W) $9^1/_2$" x 3" for Block C4, 2 rectangles (X) $9^1/_2$" x 3" for Block C4 backings, 2 rectangles (Y) $11^1/_2$" x 3" for Block D2, and 2 rectangles (Z) $11^1/_2$" x 3" for Block D2 backings.
- Cut 1 rectangle (a) 20" x 8" for hanging sleeve.

From fleece:

- Cut 1 strip $6^1/_4$" wide. From this strip, cut 4 squares (b) $6^1/_4$" x $6^1/_4$" for Block A.
- Cut 4 strips $1^3/_4$" wide. From these strips, cut 4 rectangles (c) $6^1/_4$" x $1^3/_4$", 8 rectangles (d) $8^1/_4$" x $1^3/_4$", and 4 rectangles (e) $10^1/_4$" x $1^3/_4$" for Blocks B, C, and D.

From trim fabric:

- Cut 4 strips (f) $1^1/_2$" x 23".

MAKING THE BLOCKS

*Each Block is pieced and quilted before the quilt is assembled. Follow **Piecing and Pressing**, page 87, to make blocks. **Note:** Use $^1/_4$" seam allowance to piece together blocks.*

Block A

1. Draw a diagonal line (corner to corner) on wrong side of each beige plaid square (D). With right sides together, place a beige plaid square (D) on top of a green, rust, orange, or gold plaid square (H). Stitch seam $^1/_4$" from each side of drawn line (**Fig. 1**). Trim along drawn line and press open to make 2 triangle-squares $3^5/_8$" x $3^5/_8$".

Fig. 1

2. Trim $^1/_{16}$" from **each** beige side and $^9/_{16}$" from **each** plaid side to make 2 **Unit 1** triangle-squares 3" x 3" (**Fig. 2**). Make 8 **Unit 1's** (2 of each plaid).

Fig. 2

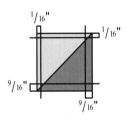

Unit 1
(make 8)

3. Repeat Step 1 using beige plaid square (B) and green, rust, orange, or gold plaid square (I) to make 2 triangle-squares $3^1/_8$" x $3^1/_8$".

4. Positioning 1 triangle-square as shown, trim $^1/_{16}$" from **each** beige side and bottom plaid side and $^9/_{16}$" from right plaid side to make a **Unit 2** rectangle $2^1/_2$" x 3" (**Fig. 3**). Make 4 **Unit 2's** (1 of each plaid).

Fig. 3

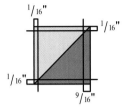

Unit 2
(make 4)

5. Positioning remaining triangle-square as shown, trim $^1/_{16}$" from **each** beige side and bottom plaid side and $^9/_{16}$" from left plaid side to make a **Unit 3** rectangle $2^1/_2$" x 3" (**Fig. 4**). Make 4 **Unit 3's** (1 of each plaid).

Fig. 4

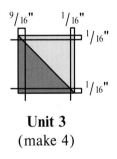

Unit 3
(make 4)

6. Sew a green, rust, orange, or gold plaid rectangle (J) and 2 beige plaid triangles (C) together as shown in **Fig. 5**. Trim to a 3" x 3" square to make **Unit 4**. Make 4 **Unit 4's** (1 of each plaid).

Fig. 5

68

Unit 4
(make 4)

7. Sew a **Unit 1**, **Unit 2**, and beige plaid square (A) together as shown to make **Unit 5**. Make 4 **Unit 5's** (1 of each plaid).

Unit 5
(make 4)

8. Sew a green, rust, orange, or gold plaid rectangle (G) and square (F) and a **Unit 3** together as shown to make **Unit 6**. Make 4 **Unit 6's** (1 of each plaid).

Unit 6
(make 4)

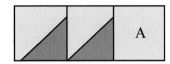

9. Sew a **Unit 4**, a green, rust, orange, or gold plaid rectangle (G), and a **Unit 1** together as shown to make **Unit 7**. Make 4 **Unit 7's** (1 of each plaid).

Unit 7
(make 4)

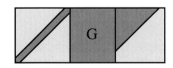

10. Sew a **Unit 5**, **Unit 6**, and **Unit 7** together as shown to make **Block A**. Make 4 **Block A's** (1 of each plaid).

Block A Diagram
(make 4)

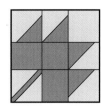

11. Follow **Quilting Instructions**, page 90, to mark **Block A's** using **Template**, page 71. Layer backing square (E), fleece square (b), and **Block A** together. Quilt on marked lines.

Blocks B1 and B2

1. Follow **Quilting Instructions**, page 90, to layer backing rectangles (L and P), fleece rectangles (c), and No. 1 and No. 2 rust plaid rectangles (K and O) together to make 2 each of **Blocks B1** and **B2**. Quilt a straight line down the center of each block.

Block B1   **Block B2**
(make 2)   (make 2)

Blocks C1, C2, C3, and C4

1. Follow **Quilting Instructions**, page 90, to layer backing rectangles (N, R, T, and X), fleece rectangles (d), and No. 1 and No. 2 rust and dark green plaid rectangles (M, Q, S, and W) together to make 2 each of **Blocks C1, C2, C3, and C4**. Quilt a straight line down the center of each block.

Block C1   **Block C2**
(make 2)   (make 2)

Block C3   **Block C4**
(make 2)   (make 2)

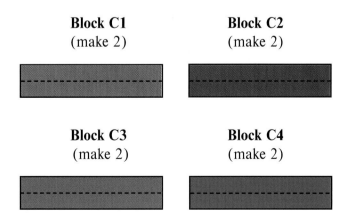

Blocks D1 and D2

1. Follow **Quilting Instructions**, page 90, to layer backing rectangles (V and Z), fleece rectangles (e), and No. 1 and No. 2 dark green plaid rectangles (U and Y) together to make 2 each of **Blocks D1** and **D2**. Quilt a straight line down the center of each block.

Block D1
(make 2)

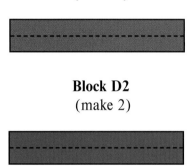

Block D2
(make 2)

ASSEMBLING THE QUILT

*As the quilt is assembled, the rag seams are created on the front of the quilt by sewing the blocks and borders together with back sides together. Refer to **Assembling The Quilt**, page 88, for additional information. Use ¹/₂" seam allowance to assemble quilt.*

1. Using 4 different colors, sew a **Block B**, 2 **Block C's**, and a **Block D** to a **Block A** in alphabetical order as shown to make **Units 8** and **9**. Make 2 **Unit 8's** and 2 **Unit 9's**.

Unit 8
(make 2)

Unit 9
(make 2)

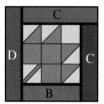
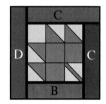

2. Sew 2 **Unit 8's** and 2 **Unit 9's** together.

Quilt Diagram

COMPLETING THE QUILT

Refer to page 89 for Steps 1-3.

1. Using rectangle (a), make and attach a hanging sleeve to back of quilt.

2. Sew trim strips (f) to edges of quilt.

3. Fringe rag seams. Wash and dry quilt.

Template

December

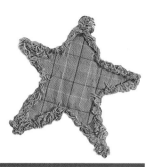

Finished Block Size: 4" x 4" (10 cm x 10 cm)
Finished Size (including outer fringe): 37" x 41" (94 cm x 104 cm)

Scrap of gold plaid
³/₄ yd (69 cm) **each** of 2 beige plaids
Scraps of 6 navy plaids
³/₈ yd (34 cm) **each** of 5 dark green plaids
¹/₄ yd (23 cm) of dark red plaid
³/₈ yd (34 cm) **each** of 6 red plaids

¹/₈ yd (11 cm) of red and green plaid
³/₈ yd (34 cm) **each** of 4 red and green plaids
1 yd (91 cm) of fleece for batting
³/₈ yd (34 cm) of hanging sleeve fabric
¹/₄ yd (23 cm) of trim fabric

CUTTING OUT THE BLOCKS AND BORDERS

Refer to **Rotary Cutting**, *page 84, before beginning project.*

From gold plaid:
- Use pattern, page 78, to cut 2 stars (A).

From each of 2 beige plaids:
- Cut 2 strips 5" wide. From these strips, cut 7 squares (B) 5" x 5" for Blocks A1 and A2, 7 squares (C) 5" x 5" for Block A1 and A2 backings, 1 rectangle (D) 3" x 5" for Block I, and 1 rectangle (E) 3" x 5" for Block I backing.
- Cut 2 strips 5³/₄" wide. From these strips, cut 8 squares 5³/₄" x 5³/₄". Cut each square once diagonally to make 8 triangles (F) for Block F and 8 triangles (G) for Block F backings.

From each of 6 navy plaids:
- Cut 1 square 5³/₄" x 5³/₄". Cut square once diagonally to make 1 triangle (H) for Block G and 1 triangle (I) for Block G backing.

From each of 5 dark green plaids:
- Cut 1 strip 5" wide. From this strip, cut 2 squares (J) 5" x 5" for Block B and 2 squares (K) 5" x 5" for Block B backings.
- Cut 1 strip 5³/₄" wide. From this strip, cut 2 squares 5³/₄" x 5³/₄". Cut each square once diagonally to make 2 triangles (L) for Block H and 2 triangles (M) for Block H backings.

From dark red plaid:
- Cut 1 strip 5" wide. From this strip, cut 1 square (N) 5" x 5" for Block C and 1 square (O) 5" x 5" for Block C backing.

From each of 6 red plaids:
- Cut 2 strips 5" wide. From these strips, cut 5 squares (P) 5" x 5" for Block D and 5 squares (Q) 5" x 5" for Block D backing.

From red and green plaid:
- Cut 1 strip 3" wide. From these strips, cut 4 squares (R) 3" x 3" for Block E and 4 squares (S) 3" x 3" for Block E backing.

From each of 2 red and green plaids:
- Cut 2 strips 5" wide. From these strips, cut 9 rectangles (T) 5" x 3" for Block J and 9 rectangles (U) 5" x 3" for Block J backings.

From each of 2 red and green plaids:
- Cut 2 strips 5" wide. From these strips, cut 8 rectangles (V) 5" x 3" for Block J and 8 rectangles (W) 5" x 3" for Block J backings.

From fleece:
- Cut 8 strips 3³/₄" wide. From these strips, cut 71 squares (X) 3³/₄" x 3³/₄" and 36 rectangles (Y) 3³/₄" x 1³/₄". Cut 16 of these squares once diagonally to make 32 triangles (Z).
- Cut 1 strip 1³/₄" wide. From this strip, cut 4 squares (a) 1³/₄" x 1³/₄".

From hanging sleeve fabric:
- Cut 1 rectangle (b) 35" x 9".

From trim fabric:
- Cut 2 strips (c) 1¹/₂" x 42".
- Cut 2 strips (d) 1¹/₂" x 38".

MAKING THE BLOCKS AND BORDERS

*Each Block and Border is pieced and quilted before the quilt is assembled. Follow **Piecing and Pressing**, page 87, to make blocks.*

Blocks A1 and A2

1. Mark 4 (2 of each plaid) beige plaid squares (B) using **Template 1**, page 78.
2. Layer beige plaid backing square (C), fleece square (X), and beige plaid square (B) together.
3. Quilt marked design to make **Block A1**. Make 4 **Block A1's**.

Block A1 Diagram

(make 4)

4. Layer remaining beige plaid backing squares (C), fleece squares (X), and beige plaid squares (B) together and quilt with an X as shown to make 10 **Block A2's** (5 of each plaid).

Block A2 Diagram

(make 10)

Block B

1. Layer dark green plaid backing square (K), fleece square (X), and dark green plaid square (J) together.
2. Quilt blocks with an X as shown to make **Block B**. Make 10 **Block B's** (2 of each plaid).

Block B Diagram

(make 10)

Block C

1. Layer dark red plaid backing square (O), fleece square (X), and dark red plaid square (N) together.
2. Quilt block with an X as shown to make **Block C**.

Block C Diagram

Block D

1. Layer red plaid backing square (Q), fleece square (X), and red plaid square (P) together.
2. Quilt block with an X as shown to make **Block D**. Make 30 **Block D's** (5 of each plaid).

Block D Diagram

(make 30)

Block E

1. Layer red and green plaid backing square (S), fleece square (a), and red and green plaid square (R) together.
2. Quilt blocks with an X as shown to make **Block E**. Make 4 **Block E's**.

Block E Diagram

(make 4)

Block F

1. Mark beige plaid triangle (F) using **Template 2**, page 78.
2. Layer beige plaid backing triangle (G), fleece triangle (Z), and beige plaid triangle (F) together.
3. Quilt marked design to make 16 **Block F's** (8 of each plaid).

Block F Diagram
(make 16)

Block G

1. Mark navy plaid triangle (H) using **Template 2**, page 78.
2. Layer navy plaid backing triangle (I), fleece triangle (Z), and navy plaid triangle (H) together.
3. Quilt marked design to make 6 **Block G's** (1 of each plaid).

Block G Diagram
(make 6)

Block H

1. Mark dark green plaid triangle (L) using **Template 2**, page 78.
2. Layer dark green plaid backing triangle (M), fleece triangle (Z), and dark green plaid triangle (L) together.
3. Quilt marked design to make 10 **Block H's** (2 of each plaid).

Block H Diagram
(make 10)

Block I

1. Layer beige plaid backing rectangle (E), fleece rectangle (Y), and beige plaid rectangle (D) together.
2. Quilt with a straight line down the center of the block to make 2 **Block I's** (1 of each plaid).

Block I Diagram
(make 2)

Block J

1. Layer red and green plaid backing rectangle (U or W), fleece rectangle (Y), and red and green plaid rectangle (T or V) together.
2. Quilt with a straight line down the center of the block to make 34 **Block J's** (9 each of 2 red and green plaids and 8 each of remaining 2 red and green plaids).

Block J Diagram
(make 34)

ASSEMBLING THE QUILT

*As the quilt is assembled, the rag seams are created on the front of the quilt by sewing the blocks and borders together with back sides together. Refer to **Assembling The Quilt**, page 88, for additional information. Use 1/2" seam allowance to assemble quilt.*

1. Sew a **Block F** and a **Block G** together as shown to make **Unit 1**. Make 6 **Unit 1's**.

Unit 1
(make 6)

2. Sew a **Block F** and a **Block H** together as shown to make **Unit 2**. Make 10 **Unit 2's**.

Unit 2

(make 10)

3. Sew 2 **Block E's** and 8 **Block J's** together as shown to make **Unit 3**. Make 2 **Unit 3's**.

Unit 3

(make 2)

4. Sew 2 **Block J's** and 8 **Block D's** together as shown to make **Unit 4**. Make 2 **Unit 4's**.

Unit 4

(make 2)

5. Sew 2 **Block J's**, 2 **Block D's**, 4 **Unit 1's**, and 2 **Block A2's** together as shown to make **Unit 5**.

Unit 5

6. Sew 2 **Block J's**, 2 **Block D's**, 2 **Unit 1's**, 2 **Block A1's**, and 2 **Unit 2's** together as shown to make **Unit 6**.

Unit 6

7. Sew **Unit 5** and **Unit 6** together. Trim excess fabric from the underneath seam allowance where blocks intersect. Follow **Frayed-Edge Appliqué**, page 91, to sew star to top of tree (**Fig. 1**).

Fig. 1

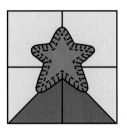

8. Sew 2 **Block J's**, 2 **Block D's**, 2 **Block A1's**, 2 **Unit 2's**, and 2 **Block B's** together as shown to make **Unit 7**.

Unit 7

9. Sew 2 **Block J's**, 2 **Block D's**, 2 **Block A2's**, 2 **Unit 2's**, and 2 **Block B's** together as shown to make **Unit 8**. Make 2 **Unit 8's**.

Unit 8

(make 2)

10. Sew 2 **Block J's**, 2 **Block D's**, 2 **Unit 2's**, and 4 **Block B's** together as shown to make **Unit 9**.

Unit 9

11. Sew 2 **Block J's**, 2 **Block D's**, 4 **Block A2's**, 2 **Block I's**, and a **Block C** together as shown to make **Unit 10**.

Unit 10

12. Sew **Units 3 - 10** together as shown.

COMPLETING THE QUILT
Refer to page 89 for Steps 1-3.
1. Using rectangle (b), make and attach a hanging sleeve to back of quilt.
2. Sew trim strips (c) to side edges of quilt. Sew trim strips (d) to top and bottom edges of quilt.
3. Fringe rag seams. Wash and dry quilt.

Quilt Diagram

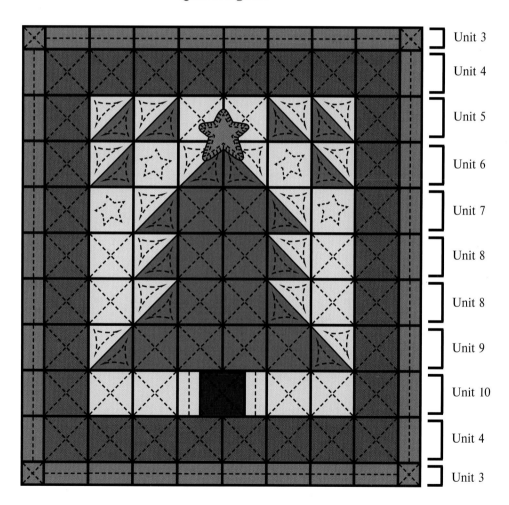

Unit 3
Unit 4
Unit 5
Unit 6
Unit 7
Unit 8
Unit 8
Unit 9
Unit 10
Unit 4
Unit 3

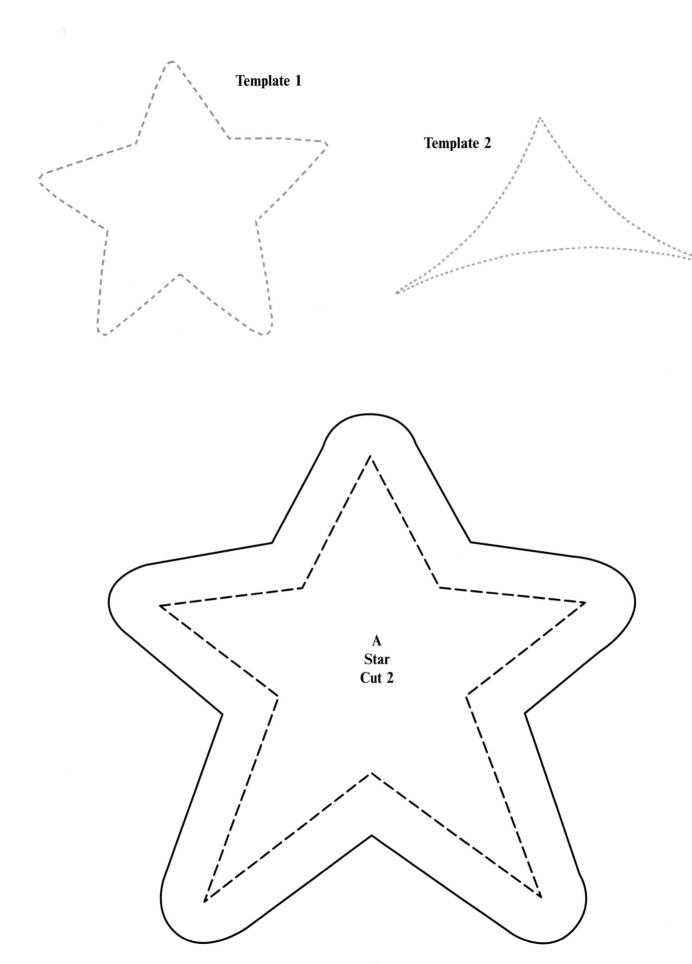

Template 1

Template 2

A
Star
Cut 2

78

MAKING A PILLOW

Many of the block patterns used for these wall quilts will work for a pillow. For example, one 12" log cabin block (**Fig. 1**) will make a 12" pillow. Use nine 5" blocks for a 15" pillow (**Fig. 2**) or four 5" blocks for a 10" pillow (**Fig. 3**). Make an 11" pillow by adding 2" borders to a block (**Fig. 4**).

Fig. 1

Fig. 2

Fig. 3

Fig. 4

1. Follow **Assembling the Quilt**, page 88, to sew the blocks together to form the pillow top.
2. Measure the pillow top. For the pillow back, cut 2 rectangles the length of the pillow top and 4" less than the width of the pillow top. For example, for a 13" square pillow top the cut size of each pillow back would be 9" x 13".

3. Press one long edge of each pillow back $^3/_8$" to wrong side. Press $^3/_8$" to wrong side again. Stitch along folded edge.
4. Overlapping hemmed edges and aligning raw edges, place the pillow top and pillow backs together, wrong sides facing. (If the hemmed edge falls on a seam, trim a small amount off the raw edge.) Pin in place.
5. Follow **General Instructions**, page 81, to add trim, fringe, wash, and dry pillow. Insert pillow form.

MAKING A LARGER QUILT

Many of the block patterns used for these wall quilts will work for larger quilts. Alternate two blocks with or without a border as shown in **Figs. 5 - 6**. Alternate groups of blocks with sashing and corner blocks as shown in **Fig. 7**. Combine several block patterns for a custom quilt.

Fig. 5

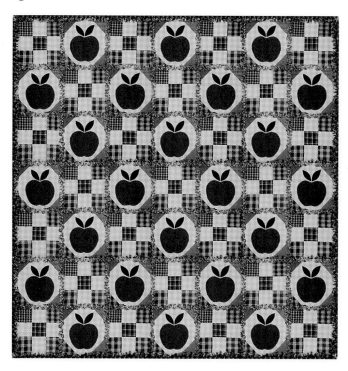

Fig. 6

Fig. 7

To figure yardage for a larger quilt, determine the number of each piece needed. This example is for fifty 5" squares.

1. Divide the usable width of the fabric (42") by the width of the piece (5") and round down to get a total of 8 pieces per width of fabric.
2. Divide the total number of pieces needed (50) by the pieces per width of fabric (8) and round up to get a total of 7 strips needed.

3. Multiply the total number of strips (7) by the length of the piece (5") to get the number of inches of fabric needed (35"). Add several inches for shrinkage and straightening (38").
4. Divide this number by 36" to get the yardage needed, rounding up to the nearest $^1/_8$ yard ($1^1/_8$ yds). Repeat for all pieces needed.

General Instructions

Complete instructions are given for making each of the quilts shown in this leaflet. To make your quilting easier and more enjoyable, we encourage you to carefully read all of the General Instructions, study the color photographs, and familiarize yourself with the individual project instructions before beginning a project.

BASIC TOOLS AND SUPPLIES

This list includes all the tools necessary to complete these projects plus additional supplies used for special techniques. Unless otherwise specified, all items may be found in your favorite fabric store or quilt shop.

CUTTING TOOLS

Rotary Cutter — The rotary cutter consists of a round blade mounted on a handle with a retractable blade guard for safety. The blade is very sharp, so keep it closed when not in use. It should be used only with a cutting mat and rotary cutting ruler. Several sizes are generally available; we recommend the 45 mm size for cutting 4 or more layers at once. Keep extra blades on hand and replace when the blade becomes dull or nicked (it no longer cuts without a lot of pressure or skips spots when cutting).

Rotary Cutting Mat — There are several sizes and brands of mats available. An 18" x 24" or 24" x 36" mat with 1" grid lines are good sizes for most cutting. After purchasing the mat, do not leave it in a hot car or in direct sunlight. It will warp and become unusable; always store flat.

Rotary Cutting Ruler — A rotary cutting ruler is a thick, clear acrylic ruler made specifically for use with a rotary cutter. Choose rulers that have accurate $1/8$" increments marked both horizontally and vertically and guidelines for 45° and 60° angles. A variety of sizes are available that make specific cutting tasks faster and easier. You may find the following sizes helpful:

- 6" x 24" rectangle — Cutting strips across the fabric width.
- 6" square — Subcutting strips, trimming pieced triangle-squares.
- $12^1/_2$" square — Cutting strips or squares larger than 6", squaring your fabric or blocks.
- 3" x 18" rectangle — Cutting squares into triangles, cutting narrow strips, marking diagonal lines for quilting.

SEWING SUPPLIES

Sewing Machine — A sewing machine that produces a good, even straight stitch and has an adjustable needle position or a presser foot that will make an exact $1/4$" seam is all that is necessary for most quilting. A machine with a lock stitch and needle up or down button is a plus. Zigzag Stitch capability is necessary for Satin Stitch Appliquéing. Keep your sewing machine in good working order, clean and oil it often, and keep the tension set properly.

Machine Needles — A size 14 needle is usually used for machine piecing and quilting.

Walking Foot (required) — Use this foot for machine piecing as well as quilting for best results. When quilting, it will help all 3 layers move at the same rate over the feed dogs to provide a smoother quilted project.

Thread — Choose a good quality cotton-covered polyester thread. You will need thread to blend with all colors for piecing (beige or tan colors work best with plaids), thread to match appliqué fabrics, and thread to match or blend with backing fabrics. If you're using a variety of fabric and want your quilting stitches to blend with the different colors, use monofilament (nylon) thread for quilting. This thread may also be used for appliqués if desired. Use a very fine (.004 mm) soft nylon thread that is not stiff or wiry. Choose clear nylon thread for white or light fabrics or smoke nylon thread for darker fabrics. Do not use nylon thread in the bobbin.

Seam Ripper — A good seam ripper with a fine point is useful for removing stitching.

Quilter's Pins — Straight pins made especially for quilting are extra long with large round heads. Glass head pins will stand up to occasional contact with a hot iron. Some quilters prefer extra-fine dressmaker's silk pins.

Scissors — Although most fabric cutting will be done with a rotary cutter, you will also need a standard pair of scissors for cutting fabric. A separate pair of scissors for cutting paper and plastic is recommended. Smaller scissors are handy for clipping threads. If you're making a lot of quilts, you may prefer to have a separate pair for fringing.

Iron and Ironing Surface — You will need an iron with both steam and dry settings, and a pressing pad or traditional ironing board. An iron with a smooth, clean soleplate is necessary for proper pressing.

Tip: If you don't have a cutting table 34"–36" high, you can easily make your own with a few supplies from your local hardware and lumber store.

You will need:
$3/4$" thick shelf — 24" x 36" **or** 24" x 48"   Four 4"-8" high hardwood legs
Four straight top plates   Sixteen $1/2$" screws
Four self-stick felt pads

Placing plates 2" from each corner, screw the plates to one side of the shelf. Place the felt pads on the bottom of the legs and screw the legs onto the plates. To use, place this on a standard 30" high table or folding table.

OTHER SUPPLIES

Template Material – There are several types of template material available for making quilting templates.

Marking Pencils – For marking blocks for quilting, we recommend disappearing or water-erasable ink for lighter colors and a white marking pencil for darker colors. A silver quilter's pencil is a good marker for both light and dark fabrics. Always test markers on fabric scraps before using them on your quilt. Do not iron marked fabrics. It may set the marks and ruin your quilt.

Small Removable Labels – Place a label on blocks or rows to keep them in order.

Fine Tip Permanent Fabric Marker – A permanent pen is used to mark quilting templates and to sign and date quilts. Test pen on fabric to make sure it will not bleed or wash out.

Paper-Backed Fusible Web – This iron-on adhesive with paper backing is used to secure fabric cut-outs to another fabric when appliquéing. For appliqué, choose a lighter-weight web that will not gum up your sewing machine needle. There are several different brands available.

Tear Away Stabilizer – This commercially made, non-woven material or paper stabilizer is used on the back of the block to keep the fabric from shifting or stretching while sewing on appliqués with a Satin Stitch.

Batting – We recommend using a good quality fleece for easier cutting but any regular or low-loft batting will work for these quilts. Fleece is available in 1 yard packages or on a bolt. If you make a lot of quilts, you probably have plenty of batting scraps that also could be used. For a thinner batting, you may also use solid-color flannel.

FABRICS

Choosing Fabric

The best fabric choices for these quilts are high-quality 100% cotton homespun plaids or some lightweight flannels. Other fabrics do not fray well. Look for fabrics that are the same color on both sides. Regular cotton prints will work for the Satin Stitch appliqués, and also for the center unit on some of the pieced blocks. The yardage requirements given for each project are based on 45" wide fabric with a "usable" width of 42" after shrinkage and trimming selvages. Our recommended yardage lengths should be adequate for occasional resquaring of fabric when many cuts are required.

Preparing Fabric

All fabric should be washed in warm water, dried, and pressed before cutting.

1. To check colorfastness before washing, cut a small piece of the fabric and place in a glass of hot water with a small amount of detergent. Leave fabric in the water for a few minutes. Remove fabric from water and blot with white paper towels. If any color bleeds onto the towels, wash the fabric separately with warm water and detergent, then rinse until the water runs clear. If fabric continues to bleed, choose another fabric.

2. Unfold yardage and separate fabrics by color. To help reduce raveling, use scissors to snip a small triangle from each corner of your fabric pieces. Machine wash fabrics in warm water with a small amount of mild laundry detergent. Do not use fabric softener. Rinse well and then dry fabrics in the dryer, checking long fabric lengths occasionally to make sure they are not tangling.

3. To make ironing easier, remove fabrics from dryer while they are slightly damp. Press each fabric using a steam iron set on "Cotton."

ROTARY CUTTING

One of the most important steps in making a quilt is cutting the pieces accurately. Plaid fabrics are more challenging to cut, especially if you want to keep the lines in the plaid straight with the seam. By following the instructions below, you should be able to cut the pieces within an $^1/_8$" of the straight line of the plaid most of the time. For more perfect cuts, you may prefer cutting them one at a time. The blocks for rag quilts are normally larger than those for traditional quilts, so there are not as many pieces to cut.

Cutting Plaid Strips

1. Using scissors, trim one end of the fabric straight with the plaid. Remove the selvage edges (**Fig. 1**). If the selvage edges are too much off grain and you don't need the full width of the fabric for your blocks, you can remove up to 2 inches off the selvage edge. This strip can be used for trim pieces or strip-pieced blocks.

Fig. 1

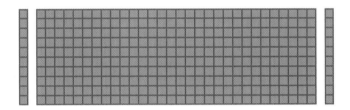

2. Refold the fabric lengthwise (as it was on the bolt) with wrong sides together. Since most homespun plaids do not have a right or wrong side, use the side of your choice.

3. All strips are cut from the selvage-to-selvage width of the fabric unless otherwise instructed. Place fabric on the cutting mat with the fold of the fabric toward you and the trimmed end on the left. Keeping the trimmed edges even, match the plaids at the selvage edge by staggering the selvage edges slightly (**Fig. 2**). Straighten the fabric if necessary by pulling on opposite diagonal corners.

Fig. 2

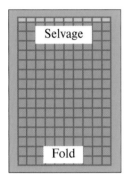

4. Fold the fabric again by bringing the folded edge up to the selvage edge, matching the plaids and keeping trimmed edges even (**Fig. 3**). The folded edge does not have to be perfectly parallel with the selvage edge. It's more important to keep the plaids matched. There will be four layers of fabric. You are now ready to cut the strips.

Fig. 3

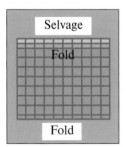

5. Place the ruler over the trimmed edge of the fabric, aligning desired marking on the ruler with the trimmed edge (**Fig. 4**). Check to make sure the right edge of the ruler is lined up as close as possible with a straight line of the plaid. Retract the blade guard on the rotary cutter, and using a smooth downward motion, make the cut by holding the ruler firmly with your left hand and running the blade of the rotary cutter firmly along the right edge of the ruler. Always cut in a direction away from your body and immediately close the blade guard after each cut. If you're cutting multiple strips from the same fabric, you may need to retrim the end of the fabric after several cuts to keep the plaid straight.

Fig. 4

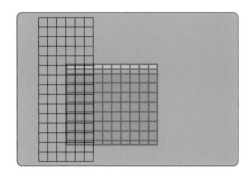

Subcutting Plaid Strips

1. Unfold the strips and lay them across the cutting surface, right side up. For faster cutting, layer up to 4 strips by lining up the selvage edges and staggering the strips slightly to line up the plaid. Using the rotary cutter, trim a small amount off the left end of the strips following the straight line of the plaid (**Fig. 5**).

Fig. 5

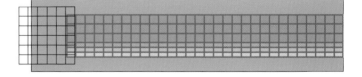

2. To cut squares or rectangles from the strips, place the ruler over the left end of strips, aligning desired marking on the ruler with the cut end of the strips. If the width is more than the size of the ruler, use the marks on the cutting mat as a guide. Cut on the straight line of the plaid (**Fig. 6**). It's okay if the blocks aren't perfectly square. They can be stretched from corner to corner to square them up. Slight imperfections will be hidden in the fringed seams.

Fig. 6

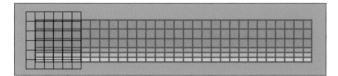

3. To cut two triangles from a square, cut a square the size indicated in the project instructions. Cut the square once diagonally to make two half-square triangles (**Fig. 7**).

Fig. 7

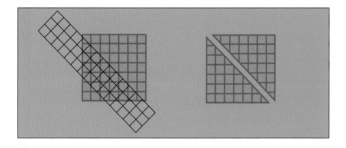

4. To cut four triangles from a square, cut a square the size indicated in the project instructions. Cut the square twice diagonally to make four quarter-square triangles (**Fig. 8**).

Fig. 8

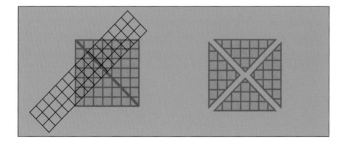

Cutting Solids or Prints

1. When working with solids or prints, fold the fabric selvage to selvage and align the selvage and folded edge as close as possible with the marks on the cutting mat. Trim the uneven edge square with the folded edge (**Fig. 9**). Fold the fabric again, keeping trimmed edges even, then cut the strips (**Fig. 10**). When cutting multiple strips from the same fabric, make sure the cuts remain at a perfect right angle to the fold. Retrim the uneven edge as needed.

Fig. 9   **Fig. 10**

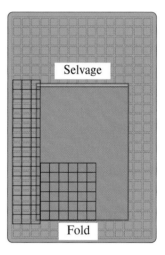
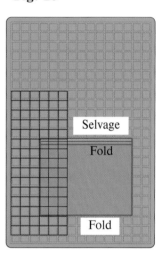

2. Subcut the strips the same as the plaid fabrics. You don't need to stagger the strips. Trim off the selvage edges square with the strip, or cut the first piece slightly larger than needed, rotate the piece and trim to the size needed. For perfectly square cuts, align a horizontal marking on the ruler with one long edge of the strip before cutting (**Fig. 11**).

Fig. 11

> **Tip:** When making quilts with multiple pieces of the same fabric, cut a few extra pieces and watch for flaws during assembly.

PIECING AND PRESSING

Precise cutting, followed by accurate piecing and careful pressing, will ensure that all the pieces of your quilt top fit together well. For best results, use a walking foot for all piecing, but be sure to use an accurate $^1/_4$" seam allowance.

Piecing

Set sewing machine stitch length for approximately 12-15 stitches per inch. Use a new, sharp needle suited for medium-weight woven fabric.

Use a neutral-colored general-purpose sewing thread (not quilting thread) in the needle and in the bobbin. Stitch first on a scrap of fabric to check upper and bobbin thread tension; make any adjustments necessary. A $^1/_4$" **seam allowance** is used for piecing units into blocks.

Chain Piecing

Chain piecing whenever possible will make your work go faster and will usually result in more accurate piecing. Stack the pieces you will be sewing beside your machine in the order you will need them and in a position that will allow you to easily pick them up. Pick up each pair of pieces, carefully place them together as they will be sewn, and feed them into the machine one after the other. Stop between each pair only long enough to pick up the next pair; don't cut thread between pairs (**Fig. 12**). After all pieces are sewn, cut threads, press, and go on to the next step, chain piecing when possible.

Fig. 12

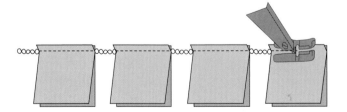

Sewing Bias Seams

Care should be used in handling and stitching bias edges since they stretch easily. After sewing the seam, carefully press seam allowance to 1 side, making sure not to stretch fabric.

Sewing Across Seam Intersections

When sewing across the intersection of 2 seams, place pieces right sides together and match seams exactly, making sure seam allowances are pressed in opposite directions (**Fig. 13**).

Fig. 13

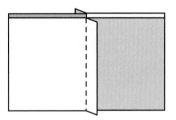

Sewing Sharp Points

To ensure sharp points when joining triangular or diagonal pieces, stitch across the center of the "X" (shown in pink) formed on the wrong side by previous seams (**Fig. 14**).

Fig. 14

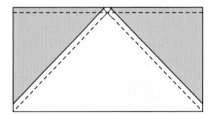

Trimming Seam Allowances

When sewing with diamond or triangle pieces, some seam allowances may extend beyond the edges of the sewn pieces. Trim away "dog ears" that extend beyond the edges of the sewn pieces (**Fig. 15**).

Fig. 15

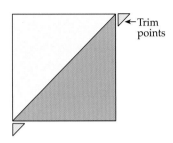

Trim points

Pressing

When making multiple-pieced blocks, plan your pressing carefully. Use a steam iron set on "Cotton" for all pressing. Set the seams before pressing by placing the iron on the stitched seam line. Press seams as you sew them, normally to one side and toward the darker fabric or in the direction that will give the least bulk, taking care to prevent small folds along seamlines. Press the seams on the right side of the fabric. When matching seams to sew rows together, seam allowances should face in opposite directions. If you accidentally press the seam in the wrong direction, repress the seam closed then press again in the opposite direction. All fringed seams **must** be pressed open.

BATTING

Although we used fleece for the batting in our projects, you can also use low-loft batting or flannel fabric. Cutting sizes for batting are given with each individual project. Use a rotary cutter and cut two layers at a time.

BACKING

The backing fabric can be the same as the block fabric or a contrasting color. Keep in mind that the seam allowance of this fabric will show on the front side of the quilt when choosing the fabric. Alternate two fabrics for a checkerboard pattern or use a variety of fabrics for a patchwork look.

ASSEMBLING THE QUILT

As the quilt is assembled, the rag seams are created on the front of the quilt by sewing the blocks and borders together with back sides together.

Set sewing machine stitch length to 12-15 stitches per inch. Lay your blocks out to form the quilt top. Using a **$^1/_2$" seam allowance**, sew into horizontal rows, sewing every other row in opposite directions. Press seams open (**Fig. 16**). Then sew rows together to finish the quilt top, alternating directions and carefully matching seams. Press remaining seams open (**Fig. 17**). To avoid bulk where multiple seams intersect, diagonally trim some of the excess fabric from the underneath seam allowance.

Fig. 16

Fig. 17

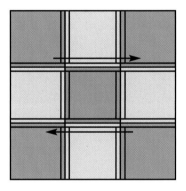

If your sewing machine skips stitches when sewing over bulky seams with a walking foot, use a regular foot for this step.

ADDING A HANGING SLEEVE

For a 3" rod pocket, cut a strip of fabric 2" less than the width of the quilt top and 8" wide; piece if necessary. To finish the short edges, press one short edge ¹/₄" to wrong side; press to wrong side again. Topstitch along folded edge. Repeat for remaining short edge. Fold the fabric in half lengthwise, right side out, and press. Baste the raw edges of the sleeve to the back of the quilt top, placing it ¹/₄" from the top edge and centering side to side. Add trim to edges, treating the hanging sleeve as part of the backing. Hand stitch the folded edge to the back of the quilt.

ADDING HANGING TABS

For tabs, cut fabric strips 3¹/₂" x 6". With right sides together and using a ¹/₄" seam allowance, sew long sides together to form a tube. Press seam open. Turn right side out. Place seam in center of back and press. Matching short ends, fold tube in half (seam to inside) and baste raw edges together. Place along top of quilt back at desired locations, with folded side down and raw edges ¹/₄" below top edge of quilt. Baste in place ³/₄" from top edge of quilt. They will be sewn while adding the first row of stitching on the trim. Fold the tabs up toward the top of the quilt before sewing the second row of stitching on the trim.

ADDING TRIM

Use matching or contrasting fabric for trim. Matching right sides and raw edges, pin the strips to the front of the quilt along the top and bottom edges. Piece if necessary by overlapping short ends ¹/₈". Stitch layers together using a ³/₄" seam allowance. Sew again ¹/₈" from the first stitching within the seam allowance (**Fig. 18**). Press strip toward the center of the quilt. Pin remaining strips to the sides of the quilt and sew in the same manner. Press toward the center of the quilt. Stitch the ends down ⁵/₈" from the edge of the quilt, backstitching at the beginning and end of each seam (**Fig. 19**).

FRINGING RAG SEAMS

Clipping to but not through the stitching line and cutting no more than two layers of fabric at a time, clip the seam allowances on each seam and the edges of the quilt ¹/₄" to ³/₈" apart. Where the seam allowances are held down by stitching, clip ¹/₈" from the seamline. Avoid cutting through pieced seams within the seam allowance by cutting at least ¹/₈" away from the seam. Diagonal seams should be left uncut within ¹/₄" of the seamline. Clip corners as shown (**Fig. 20**). Start cutting with the last seams sewn and work toward the first seams sewn.

Fig. 20

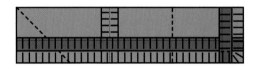

WASHING AND DRYING

Shake the quilt outside before placing in the washer. If possible, use a washer with a lint trap. Shake the quilt outside again before placing in the dryer. Dry quilt in the dryer. Check the dryer for lint during the cycle. Shake the quilt outside again after removing from the dryer. Trim excess fabric at corners if needed. Use the sticky side of masking tape to remove any remaining threads. You may need to wash and dry your quilt more than once to get the desired results. If making multiple projects, you may wish to wash several small quilts at the same time.

Tip: Rag quilts make a lot of lint! When fringing the quilts, keep a vacuum cleaner handy and avoid wearing clothing that attracts lint.

Fig. 18

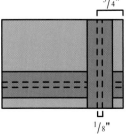

Fig. 19

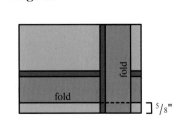

Quilting Instructions

MAKING A TEMPLATE

To make a template of the quilting pattern, center template plastic over pattern and use a permanent marker to trace pattern onto plastic. Use a craft knife with a single or double blade to cut narrow slits along traced lines (**Fig. 21**).

Fig. 21

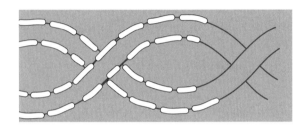

MARKING THE QUILT BLOCKS

Fabric marking pencils, various types of chalk markers, and fabric marking pens with inks that disappear with exposure to air or water are readily available and work well for different applications. White pencils work well on dark-color fabrics, and silver pencils show up well on many colors. Since chalk rubs off easily, it's a good choice if you are marking as you quilt. Fabric marking pens make more durable and visible markings, but the marks should be carefully removed according to manufacturer's instruction. Press down only as hard as necessary to make a visible line. To choose marking tools, test different markers on scrap fabric until you find the one that gives the best result.

Use desired marking tool and stencil to mark quilting lines onto the center front of the quilt block about $^1/_2$" inside the seam allowance (1" from the outside edge on fringed seams) to compensate for the fringe covering the edge of the block. For faster quilting, mark plain blocks with an X (**Fig. 22**) and narrow rectangle blocks with a straight line down the center (**Fig. 23**).

Fig. 22   **Fig. 23**

LAYERING THE BLOCKS

Center the batting on the wrong side of the backing fabric (**Fig. 24**). Place the quilt block on top (right side up) and pin in place (**Fig. 25**), keeping the pins away from the marked lines.

Fig. 24   **Fig. 25**

QUILTING THE BLOCKS

Set your sewing machine stitch length to 10-12 stitches per inch. Use matching or contrasting thread or nylon thread to blend with all fabrics. When using nylon thread, loosen the upper thread tension to keep the bobbin thread from showing on top of the quilt. For best results, use a walking foot.

Much of the quilting in the projects is "in-the-ditch." Quilting very close to the seamline is called "in-the-ditch" quilting. Quilt on the side opposite the seam allowance.

If the quilting pattern you have chosen does not go into the corner of the blocks (Example: Quilting "in the ditch" on nine patch blocks), quilt across the corners as shown in **Fig. 26**, about 2" from the corner through batting and backing only. This will prevent the batting from shifting in the corners during washing.

Fig. 26

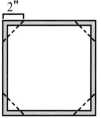

Appliqué Instructions

Note: *If the appliqué pattern you have chosen does not go into the corner of the blocks, refer to **Quilting Instructions, Fig. 26**, for quilting across the corners to prevent the batting from shifting during washing.*

FRAYED-EDGE APPLIQUÉ

Trace the desired appliqué pattern on a piece of paper and cut out. Use pattern to cut two appliqué pieces from same fabric for each appliqué.

Place paper-backed fusible web, web side down, over desired appliqué pattern. Use a pencil to trace pattern onto paper side of web following the dashed line; cut out.

Follow manufacturer's instructions to fuse traced pattern to wrong side of one of the appliqué pieces, centering it on the fabric. Remove paper backing. Place the remaining appliqué piece on top, wrong sides together, lining it up carefully; fuse in place.

Layer the block with backing and batting. Center the appliqué on the block and pin in place. Use a triple stitch to sew the appliqué in place using the size seam allowance marked on the appliqué pattern. See **Tip**, page 26. To fringe, clip the seam allowances $^1/_4$" to $^3/_8$" apart.

SATIN STITCH APPLIQUÉ

Place paper-backed fusible web, web side down, over desired appliqué pattern. Use a pencil to trace pattern onto paper side of web as many times as indicated in project instructions for a single fabric. Cut out, leaving a small border.

Follow manufacturer's instructions to fuse traced patterns to wrong side of fabrics. Do not remove paper backing. Use scissors to cut out appliqué pieces along traced lines. Remove paper backing from all pieces. Centering design on the block, fuse in place. Layer the block with backing and batting. Appliqué with Satin Stitch, using a stabilizer on the back of the block.

SATIN STITCH

1. Thread needle of sewing machine with general purpose thread that coordinates or contrasts with appliqué fabric and use thread that matches background fabric in the bobbin. Loosen the upper thread tension to keep the bobbin thread from showing on top of the quilt. Set sewing machine for a medium width (approximately $^1/_8$") zigzag stitch and a very short stitch length. Begin by stitching 2 or 3 stitches in place to anchor thread. Most of the zigzag stitch should be done on the appliqué with the right edges of the stitch falling at the very outside edge of the appliqué. Stitch over all exposed raw edges of appliqué pieces.

2. (**Note:** Dots on **Figs. 27-32** indicate where to leave needle in fabric when pivoting.) For **outside corners**, stitch just past the corner, stopping with the needle in **background** fabric (**Fig. 27**). Raise presser foot. Pivot project, lower presser foot, and stitch adjacent side (**Fig. 28**).

Fig. 27   **Fig. 28**

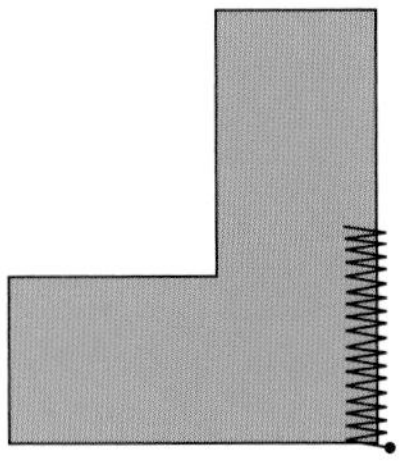

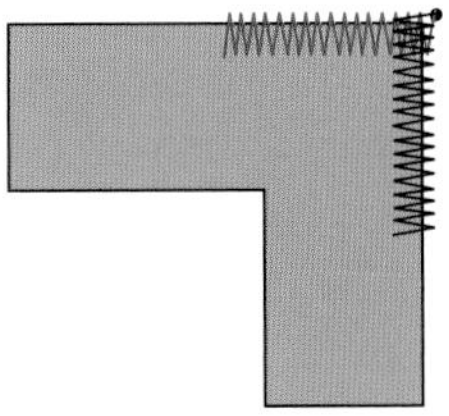

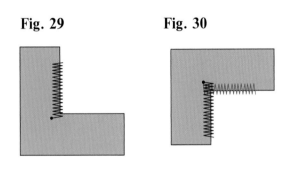

3. For **inside corners**, stitch just past the corner, stopping with the needle in **appliqué** fabric (**Fig. 29**). Raise presser foot. Pivot project, lower presser foot, and stitch adjacent side (**Fig. 30**).

Fig. 29   **Fig. 30**

4. When stitching **outside** curves, stop with needle in **background** fabric. Raise presser foot and pivot project as needed. Lower presser foot and continue stitching, pivoting as often as necessary to follow curve (**Fig. 31**).

Fig. 31

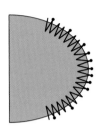

5. When stitching **inside curves**, stop with needle in **appliqué** fabric. Raise presser foot and pivot project as needed. Lower presser foot and continue stitching, pivoting as often as necessary to follow curve (**Fig. 32**).

Fig. 32

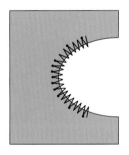

6. Do not backstitch at end of stitching. Pull threads to wrong side of background fabric; knot thread and trim ends.
7. Carefully tear away stabilizer.

Glossary

Appliqué — A cutout fabric shape that is secured to a larger background. Also refers to the technique of securing the cutout pieces.

Backing — The back or bottom layer of a quilt, sometimes called the "lining."

Backstitch — A reinforcing stitch taken at the beginning and end of a seam to secure stitches.

Batting — The middle layer of a quilt; provides the insulation and warmth as well as the thickness.

Bias — The diagonal (45° for true bias) grain of fabric in relation to crosswise or lengthwise grain (see **Fig. 33**).

Border — Strips of fabric that are used to frame a quilt top.

Chain piecing — A machine-piecing method consisting of joining pairs of pieces one after the other by feeding them through the sewing machine without cutting the thread between the pairs.

Grain — the direction of the threads in woven fabric. "Crosswise grain" refers to the threads running from selvage to selvage. "Lengthwise grain" refers to threads running parallel to the selvages (**Fig. 33**).

Fig. 33

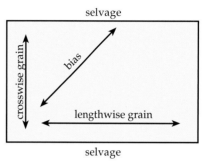

Piecing — Sewing together the pieces of a quilt design to form a quilt block or an entire quilt top.

Quilt block – Pieced or appliquéd sections that are sewn together to form a quilt top.

Quilt top – The decorative part of a quilt that is layered on top of the batting and backing.

Quilting – The stitching that holds together the 3 quilt layers (top, batting, and backing); or, the entire process of making a quilt.

Sashing – Strips or blocks of fabric that separate individual blocks in a quilt top.

Seam allowance – The distance between the seam and the cut edge of the fabric. In quilting, this is usually $1/4$".

Selvages – The 2 finished lengthwise edges of fabric (see **Fig. 33**). Selvages should be trimmed from fabric before cutting.

Set (or Setting) – The arrangement of the quilt blocks as they are sewn together to form the quilt top.

Setting squares – Squares of plain (unpieced) fabric set between pieced or appliquéd quilt blocks in a quilt top.

Setting triangles – Triangles of fabric used around the outside of a diagonally-set quilt top to fill in between outer squares and border or binding.

Stencil – A pattern used for marking quilting lines.

Straight grain – The crosswise or lengthwise grain of fabric (see **Fig. 33**). The lengthwise grain has the least amount of stretch.

Strip set – Two or more strips of fabric that are sewn together along the long edges, and then cut apart across the width of the sewn strips to create smaller units.

Template – A pattern used for marking quilt pieces to be cut out.

Unit – A pieced section that is made as individual steps in the quilt construction process are completed. Units are usually combined to make blocks or other sections of the quilt top.

Notes

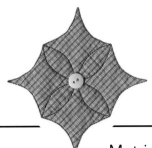

Metric Conversion Chart

Inches x 2.54 = centimeters (cm)
Inches x 25.4 = millimeters (mm)
Inches x .0254 = meters (m)

Yards x .9144 = meters (m)
Yards x 91.44 = centimeters (cm)
Centimeters x .3937 = inches (")
Meters x 1.0936 = yards (yd)

Standard Equivalents

1/8"	3.2 mm	0.32 cm	1/8 yard	11.43 cm	0.11 m
1/4"	6.35 mm	0.635 cm	1/4 yard	22.86 cm	0.23 m
3/8"	9.5 mm	0.95 cm	3/8 yard	34.29 cm	0.34 m
1/2"	12.7 mm	1.27 cm	1/2 yard	45.72 cm	0.46 m
5/8"	15.9 mm	1.59 cm	5/8 yard	57.15 cm	0.57 m
3/4"	19.1 mm	1.91 cm	3/4 yard	68.58 cm	0.69 m
7/8"	22.2 mm	2.22 cm	7/8 yard	80 cm	0.8 m
1"	25.4 mm	2.54 cm	1 yard	91.44 cm	0.91 m